"*Healing Racism Within* is a smart and clear-eyed book, necessary for these times. Brett Bevell transforms his own negative childhood racial experiences into psychologically constructive exercises for us to heal the inner psycho-spiritual landscape of how systemic racism manifests, not only through unjust laws and policies, but in all levels of our being." —Mike Dooley, cofounder of TUT and author of *Infinite Possibilities*

"Many people who enjoy what is being called White Privilege are waking up to a world that is holding a mirror to those whose reflection is unflattering and increasingly untenable. The stages for addressing this discouraging news, even among the best of us, generally go something like this: obliviousness, denial, awareness, guilt, immobilization, effective action. *Healing Racism Within* is a potent guide for moving into effective action—first as an inside job and then as you make your imprint on the world." —Donna Eden and David Feinstein, PhD, creators of the Eden Energy Medicine and Radiant Circuits methods and authors of *Energy Medicine: Balancing Your Body's Energies for Optimal Health, Joy and Vitality*, and many other books

"From a deep place within his heart, Brett Bevell is supporting us in realizing that racism exists, not only through unjust laws and the dysfunctional systemic policies in our businesses, schools, and government, but also in our cells, our emotions, our brains and hearts, the ghosts of our ancestors, and the family systems we've inherited—and like other forms of disease, it can be addressed and healed if we look at it fiercely and honestly, and have the courage to act accordingly. Thank you, Brett, for this beautiful bag of tools we can use to dismantle race-based conditioning." —Iyanla Vanzant, host of talk show *Iyanla: Fix My Life* and author of *One Day My Soul Just Opened Up*, *Get Over It!*, and many other books

"*Healing Racism Within* is the perfect book for these times! Taking a step beyond the important work of *White Fragility* and other books that highlight the problem, this book offers powerful exercises for us to do our own healing—personally and communally. Brett Bevell writes brilliantly of his own struggles to overcome the darkness of his upbringing and in those stories, as well as the exercises, inspires readers to do the deep work necessary to emerge into the light that heals the wounds of prejudice." —John Perkins, author of *The New Confessions of an Economic Hit Man*, *Touching the Jaguar*, and many other books

"Brett Bevell always brings his whole self into his books—his history, his pain, his wisdom, his honesty, his bedrock belief in the possibility for all of us to transform our pain into purpose. As a white person, I appreciate how he challenges me—both with urgency and with compassion—to confront my white privilege; to own my collusion, through denial and silence, with our country's racist history. What makes this book different and exciting are the exercises that Bevell includes as ways of exploring and confronting and changing what lies deep within. This book is an important addition to the growing library of anti-racism books that are finally a part of American literature." —Elizabeth Lesser, cofounder of Omega Institute and author of *Cassandra Speaks* and *Broken Open*

"As I finished this superb book, I felt the shimmering and essential power of hope and possibility—which is one of the many gifts Bevell brings to all of his work as a divine Energy Master. *Healing Racism Within* is an innovative map, guiding us through his personal experiences and offering potent, imaginative exercises to courageously address our wounds and the taboos surrounding internalized racism, and in the process initiate and deepen individual and collective healing." —Bridgit Dengel Gaspard, LCSW, author of *The Final 8th: Enlist Your Inner Selves to Accomplish Your Goals*

"The focus of this insightful book is about healing, not the guilt of wrongdoing or negative thoughts. Bevell provides numerous exercises based on Reiki's healing energy that can transform societal and generational pain into understanding and healing. The perfect book for twenty-first-century energy healing." —Monique Chapman, intuitive consultant and host of the podcast *Get Over It!*

"We've been in discussions about race for decades but *Healing Racism Within* gives us concrete actions to rewire the unwanted thinking, language, and energy of internalized racism. Beginning with seeing white privilege as a form of white cowardice, Brett Bevell has asked himself the deepest questions that then also allow me to do the same when I actively follow his framework towards change. We all need this book." —Diane Farr, actress and author of *The Girl Code*

HEALING RACISM WITHIN

A LIGHTWORKER'S GUIDE

BRETT BEVELL

Monkfish Book Publishing Company
Rhinebeck, NY

Paperback ISBN 978-1-948626-71-2
eBook ISBN 978-1-948626-46-0

Library of Congress Cataloging-in-Publication Data

Names: Bevell, Brett, author.
Title: Healing racism within : a lightworker's guide / Brett Bevell.
Description: Rhinebeck, NY : Monkfish Book Publishing Company, [2021]
Identifiers: LCCN 2021023057 (print) | LCCN 2021023058 (ebook) | ISBN
  9781948626712 (paperback) | ISBN 9781948626460 (ebook)
Subjects: LCSH: Bevell, Brett--Childhood and youth. | Racism--United
  States--Psychological aspects. | Psychic trauma--Alternative
  treatment--United States. | Reiki (Healing system) | Spiritual healing.
  | United States--Race relations--Psychological aspects.
Classification: LCC E185.625 .B48 2021 (print) | LCC E185.625 (ebook) |
  DDC 305.800973--dc23
LC record available at https://lccn.loc.gov/2021023057
LC ebook record available at https://lccn.loc.gov/2021023058

Book and cover design by Colin Rolfe
Cover photograph by Koshu Kunii
Hands illustration by Pikisuperstar

Monkfish Book Publishing Company
22 E. Market St., Suite 304
Rhinebeck, NY 12572
(845) 876-4861
monkfishpublishing.com

★ ✦ ✹

For my wife Helema and my son Dylan—
the love for I have for you both is immeasurable.
Our love is the garden in which this book was grown.

★ ✦ ✹

CONTENTS

✶ ✦ ✹

Most people know me as an energy healer. My books on the subject have been published in several languages, and I teach energy healing at the world-renowned Omega Institute as well as offer energy-healing immersions on the Soulvana app by Mindvalley. I get many compliments regarding my work in Reiki and other energy healing modalities via email and social media from people all over the world. My books typically explore cutting-edge techniques, ways to expand energy healing outside of the typical session between a practitioner and client and bring energy healing into all aspects of our lives.

However, few people know that the genesis of my work was my search for a way to heal myself from a deeply traumatic childhood. I created new techniques because the ones I was taught were not healing me fast enough. My books, and the techniques I offer through them, are always about things I've done to heal myself. These techniques were born out of necessity because I had too much psycho-spiritual baggage to heal using the typical means of talk therapy and twelve-step groups, which, although very useful, could not begin to touch the core damage done to my soul as a child.

I was born into a very dysfunctional family—one that included pedophiles, alcoholics, rapists, and murderers. Some of these people also happened to be very racist. The psychological damage I received as a child, and into my teenage years as well, could easily have caused me to become a drug addict or end up in prison. I credit the magic of Reiki and other forms of energy healing with steering my life in a more benevolent direction. This incredible healing journey has included deep introspection and sifting through my emotion landscape with the same care that an archeologist digs through the ruins of an ancient city, and through it I have come to see how the patterns of abuse, from which I have worked so hard to heal, are in many ways very similar to the patterns that exist on the grand social scale regarding racism. The issues of silence, repressed emotions, and the inability to speak openly about horrific crimes are systems I initially noticed as someone who was healing as an incest survivor. Eventually, once I was courageous enough to come face to face with how horrific my childhood was—it included witnessing a race-based murder when I was a toddler—I saw clearly how the psycho-spiritual dynamics of racism and sexual trauma were in many ways almost identical.

I found that the work I was doing to heal myself of the scars of incest and undo my psychological/emotional bonds to the perpetrators could also be used to liberate me from the same racist conditioning that had scarred and poisoned my psyche as a child. I am not saying that all racists are sexual abuse survivors, but the tools I learned working on my own healing process as a sexual abuse survivor became the same tools that helped me to see my own participation in a system of silence, denial, and oppression of others due to the color of their skin.

The chapters and exercises that follow in this book are meant to help individuals work through and release their own racist conditioning. I believe anyone can benefit from reading this book. Yet it is mostly written for those souls who have been conditioned and trained not to see racism within the society at large; the long-established institutions, laws, and norms created by white colonialism; nor themselves—those supposedly divine souls born of a culture that embraced whites as a superior race, but who now are stuck in that prism of light, chained to their own wounds and the wounds of their ancestors' errors.

It is my belief that without this work we will never truly come to terms with the racism of our collective past, nor will we be able to fully transform it into justice and fairness. This is not to imply that the only work necessary for real social change is internal. In fact, much of it needs to happen externally, through organizing, protesting, voting, and actively working for changes to our laws and institutions. But without the internal work, I fear the outer changes will never ripen to the true level of transformation we need. So I offer my experiences and wisdom in the hope that it will help create a better world for all.

Portions of this book are memories of my own history and moments of transformation, yet most of this book is written in the form of exercises that I have found very effective for my own transformation. In no way do I expect this book to be the end of the conversation on race; rather, I hope that it is simply the start of uncovering the deep emotional wounds that hold racist behavior in place. The transformational experience offered through this book can happen if you commit with courage to these exercises, allowing the ones that work for you to become a daily practice and letting go of the ones that do not resonate with you. May you discover within this book a path to begin changing yourself from the inside out. If enough of us engage in this kind of work, it will eventually change our world as a whole.

CHAPTER 1

THE WOUND WE CANNOT SEE

★ ★ ✖

During my childhood and even into my teenage years I refused to acknowledge that some members of my family were alcoholics and others were even pedophiles. Nor did I consider Clyde, my father's raging, hateful real-estate friend who bragged to us many times about having killed an innocent Black boy years before—and was someone I hated, whose presence I dreaded—to be a murderer. I never realized that by sending me and my older brother on fishing trips with Clyde, my own father let us sit alone in a boat on a lake with a murderer many times. And while I didn't like the grand wizard of the Ku Klux Klan who came to repair our television because I could see the crack of his ass hanging out while he bent over to work and I found his constant anti-Semitic commentary idiotic, it never occurred to me that my father might be a supporter of that same hateful ideology.

Even when my father spoke about wanting to put a statue of Adolf Hitler in the parking lot of his store, I told myself it was just because he was drinking, and I never attributed his vile ideas to be based on real hatred existing in his heart. In all these instances, I made excuses, not doing the deep work required of honestly confronting people, but instead creating reasons in my mind why these were good people who somehow had simply gone astray, temporarily. I hoped they would find their senses. But I was lying very deeply to myself—not because I was stupid, but because it was what I had to do to survive. In order not to go completely mad as a child trapped in this hellish environment, I had to create excuses to make my own life seem sane.

I often think our predominately white culture does the same thing with regard to its ancestry and history. For many of us, to think at the collective level of our great-great-grandparents as possible rapists and murderers—people who stole the freedom, dignity, and lives of others on a grand and inhuman scale—would not be that different from acknowledging having a parent who was in Hitler's SS. The kind of mental/emotional gymnastics one needs to undergo to pretend it was somehow all right for our culture to willingly participate in atrocities is extraordinary, and yet while growing up, we learn to do this and to do it very well. We learn it the same way that families convince themselves that a perpetrator of childhood sexual abuse among them is not performing the evil act they all know on some level is happening.

This collective denial is unhealthy, immoral, and also, unfortunately, very common. In many ways, it occurs because we rarely know the path of courage that is required to break the cycle. No one teaches us how to speak out with wisdom and courage against the ones we are supposed to love—those who raised us, fed us, and may have had some aspect of light inside of themselves, but who sided with evil, nevertheless. It is a wound we cannot see, at least not most of us. We have not been taught how to see it. We do not have the emotional skills to see it. When the rare person who does points us toward that path, rather than undergo the emotional revolution that needs to occur internally for us to do that work, we often rage against that person and outcast them—the same way millions of NFL fans raged against Colin Kaepernick for simply taking a knee to bring attention to the continued murderous injustice committed by police against people of color. Instead of killing or removing a diseased part of ourselves, we resort to killing or treating as outcasts those who are asking us to do that deep inner work.

It is important to note and acknowledge this: truly undoing racism on the personal psycho-spiritual level is deep, painful work. It is not so easy to transform society simply by changing laws and policies, though I strongly believe that those changes must happen. The deeper work—the soul cleansing, mind-shifting work—needs to happen at a deeper level. Systemic racism is hard-wired not only into our laws, our social constructs, and our institutions, but also into our cellular, ancestral memory—and as an energy healer I saw that it is also hard-wired into the mental body, emotional, and karmic bodies as well as the energy field of every human being who willingly participates in such evil.

The sacred detox process that needs to happen in order for us to clear ourselves of this hateful blight goes far beyond changing municipal budgets to spend more on community and less on police (although I do agree with that). It also goes far beyond needing to pay reparations (although I do personally think such reparations are necessary to achieve actual justice and true healing). True healing must involve a psycho-spiritual component; otherwise, the shadow of racism, the unexamined part of our collective psyche will find some way to resurrect the ugly evil of white supremacy and make it appear attractive to those who have not done this inner work. The cycle will play itself out over and over again, with only mild progressive change occurring, only to be undone later by reactionary forces that are themselves an expression of the unresolved trauma of being descendants of a culture that committed unthinkable crimes.

Knowing that our ancestors, collectively if not entirely individually, committed horrible atrocities is a terrible trauma in the same way that knowing that our parents or grandparents are pedophiles or murderers is traumatic. I am not saying this to bring pity to myself as a white person or to compare the trauma of being white with the trauma of being a person of color. In no way do I intend that comparison. What I am saying is that, when looked from a humanistic standpoint, the pain and suffering of knowing that many white ancestors committed rape, genocide, murder, and other crimes of hate under the umbrella of white supremacy is a wound many white people carry and yet cannot see. To truly undo racism, that shadow and collective pain must be witnessed and worked through. It is for our own individual liberation to do this work, as well as for the liberation of society as a whole. There is trauma there, and it is our obligation to work on it, resolve it, and be transformed by the grief, loss, and sorrow that any child can tell you is there for us until we are taught to no longer see it.

I say this from experience: this wound we cannot see exists in liberals as much as it does in any conservative. I learned this lesson very clearly in 1999, when, as part of my master's thesis, I created a piece of performance art openly confronting the atrocities committed by my family, including witnessing a Black man being murdered when I was a toddler. This piece featured a series of poems read aloud in a ritual setting as well as the initiation of the audience into Reiki energy healing to deepen the performance's spiritual detox aspect.

When I performed the ritual live before a private, selected audience, I got great support and felt as if the performance itself was equal to many thousands of dollars in therapy. I literally had a hard time speaking for a few weeks after the performance because such a rewiring of my mind had happened in the ceremonial performance; it was as if years of shame and guilt had been washed away during the one-hour event. As a writer, it was strange to be searching for words. My brain seemed suddenly different, more open, more alive, but having to struggle to find the right words when speaking to others.

I received glowing praise from the thesis committee, who told me I did not have to defend my thesis given how outstanding the performance was. Yet when I began sharing these same poems in public at open mic readings in San Francisco for hip, neo-beat, white poets, I was ostracized, called a "white-trash poet," and even eliminated from a reading I was originally supposed to be part of at the North Beach Public Library.

As painful as that time was for me, I was able to see how afraid these other poets were of my clear and detailed exposé of the race-based murder I had witnessed. It triggered something in them that made them willingly blacklist me, something I never expected from this left-leaning crowd. They could drop names like Dr. Martin Luther King and Malcolm X as easily as dropping a tab of acid, yet they were furious at me for exposing in detail a hate crime that I had witnessed as a very young boy.

Yet I should not say that all of these poets treated me horribly. Although many did, some came up to me privately and thanked me. I especially remember one poet named Anna who confided that her father had been in the Ku Klux Klan, and how the poems I read allowed her to more openly confront her own racist family past. But still, the majority of the poets either expressed open disdain of me or were silent and complicit over several months as the blacklisting of me and my work unfolded. It was not until my poem "America Needs a Buddhist President" aired nationally on NPR's *All Things*

Considered on March 29, 2000, that I suddenly was welcomed back into San Francisco's community of poets again. But by then, I no longer cared to be part of their community.

I had a short taste of provincial fame for being on NPR, when the poets all wanted to be near me, as if my short-term fame would rub off me onto them. But their ostracization turned out to be a blessing for me. It had shown me the collective psychic shadow of these poets—a shadow I believe exists for the majority of white America, born of a complete inability to deal with the deeper psycho-spiritual components of what it means to heal racism in our country. In white America, there is an inability to stare into the abyss of hundreds of years of collective pain and realize that it isn't just the George Wallaces of the world who are seething with anger and words of hatred—but that they themselves also nurse a slippery, well-educated hatred that marches for the right causes, reads the right books, is as politically correct as possible, but is really just as hateful.

I realized that for our country to ever really shed the sin of racism, our hearts, not just our minds, need healing. The white poets I knew could all give proper lip service to "the cause," but their words came out sideways. Suddenly, they were chuckling at an inappropriate joke and offering to buy me lattes. And I did accept those lattes too; they were like coins of silver, but I had to go vomit in the restroom the moment the cup touched my lips because I remembered that man whose name I did not know, but whose image I shall never forget. But this is how we agree collectively to forget about our collective crimes: through a handshake, a laugh, a drink. It's all so subtle, so easy, and nobody ever has to state openly that we are agreeing to a cover-up of pain, history, and our own humanity. We become buried in our own white lies.

UNITY CONSCIOUSNESS AND TRANSFORMING COWARDICE INTO COURAGE

★   ✦   ✶

y work as an energy healer has included many profound mystical experiences that confirm for me that we are all one human race, all aspects of the Divine expressing itself through our collective and individual human experience. What also coexists inside this unity and oneness are the complexity of the human experience, the failures and errors of our ancestors, and the social constructs through which we either accept and own those errors, learning and growing from them, or deny and repress those errors, thus allowing them to continue unaddressed and unredeemed. Unfortunately, though, there is a trend of spiritual bypassing which often occurs in the realm of energy healing, with unity and oneness emphasized to the point of excluding some very real facts of human history. The inability among those in my field of expertise to address the deep collective suffering colonialism has caused for many indigenous people over the past five hundred years is one primary example.

We who call ourselves healers or lightworkers are often color-blind in our pursuit of union with the Divine. We are all human souls, yet we often deny that each soul's experience has been filtered through the lens of their racial and cultural history, generational trauma, and the systemic racism that is ingrained throughout society. If we think of the soul as Divine light, the light that we are, then we must also acknowledge that light comes through us into the world of experience via the prism of historical truth. When light moves through a prism, that field of unity is reflected in various colors. Though we are coming from oneness, we are each different. Our light shines through the prism of historical truth, and each soul's experiences depend on their race.

The term "white privilege" is often used to describe the economic and social advantages a soul has when born into a white body. But though my own political leanings are quite far to the left, I have never been comfortable with that term, mainly because it doesn't go deep enough to allow space for real racial healing. It infers a reality that cannot change or evolve—as if those with white ancestry are somehow automatically blessed with inherent advantages that will forever be fixed and constant.

The word *privilege* connotes a sense of wealth and ease, so "white privilege" implies that all who are born white in this culture have an easy life. But that isn't always true. I do not think it was a privilege for me to be raped, abused, beaten, and forced to watch a Black man be killed when I was a toddler, but, for me, those experiences were a huge part of being born into and growing up within a white family. Nonetheless, I can acknowledge that I have advantages in society because I am white, regardless of my personal history. But those advantages exist because white society as a whole has been too emotionally disabled and lacking in the courage to come to terms with the atrocities of our collective history—to look at our past and wrestle with it until we are free of it. If we name it as the collective cowardice it is, there will be at least some incentive for white culture to change. But if we call it privilege, despite people giving long intellectual dissertations about how much change is needed, in their hearts they will not want real change—because who wants to give up their privileges? Call it cowardice, and you can inspire people to transform that cowardice into courage.

I am not saying each individual who is white is a coward in their personal life. What I am saying is that as a collective we have not been willing to face the painful shadow of our collective past, primarily when it comes to the psycho-spiritual work of addressing a history of genocide and slavery. Therefore, collectively, white cowardice is very real. Collective white cowardice creates the conditions of white privilege. White privilege is, in turn, a social symptom of the deeper social disease of white cowardice.

How does white cowardice manifest? In silence, in not speaking out when we see social injustice. White cowardice also occurs when a white person gives another person a job because they are white, although a better candidate of color has applied. You may call that racism or prejudice (which it is), but in my experience, at the deepest level it is cowardice—a fear of the other, an inability to dare to examine one's own prejudices or racial bias. And that core fear, that terror is what holds our collective racial biases in place.

The people with whom I grew up, who were the face of racism, were also cowards at the deepest level. It was cowardly for my father's friend Clyde to kill an unarmed Black boy. There was no bravery in that act. History also proves white supremacists to be cowards. The act of group lynching is cowardly. The 1963 Birmingham church bombing, which killed four young girls, was cowardly. Slavery itself was complete cowardice, for a whole culture felt too weak to be self-sustainable and thrive without having to steal other people from halfway across the planet to perform free labor. Chaining those enslaved human beings because of fear of their rightful vengeance was cowardice.

The whole history of slavery is cowardly to the core, at every step. It is time to change this cowardice into courage. In order to do this, we need to focus the issue at a deeper level than the term "white privilege." With white privilege, it is so easy to keep the argument in the mental sphere, to bypass the underlying stench of pain and suffering that is at the root of our culture; to say, "I am trying to see my place of privilege," is very different than saying, "My ancestors were cowards and the present culture that has continued their values is cowardly, and I am committed to finding the courage to face these crimes and transform them for the highest good of all."

Privilege is not a sin, but cowardice is. To put our world back in order, we need a language that addresses the real level of the psycho-spiritual damage that has occurred over the past five hundred years. And when looking at this situation from a spiritual perspective of unity consciousness, how can the souls who exist in a white body not want to find the courage in themselves to right the spiritual sins of our ancestors? If we truly believe in oneness, the desire to liberate ourselves should be burning inside each of us and inspire us to find and live from that courage. May the work in the chapters that follow bring that courage to light in your mind, your emotions, your energy body, and beyond into your actions.

Here is a healing prayer, which you can recite or see as a healing poem if the term prayer is uncomfortable.

Dear Higher Self—
Today we honor our ancestors
We acknowledge the positive and the negative
The joy, and wisdom
The errors and ignorance
The evil and cowardice
With the love that heals all things
Even the love that is beyond our own personal ability
*   to love*
The love that is beyond any one heart or person
The love that created the universe itself
We send it through time
To heal the sorrows
Mend the laws
Right the fault lines in our ancestors' perceptions so that
*   they are healed within us*
To begin the journey forward
We also ask forgiveness from any beings harmed by our
*   ancestors*
We manifest this truth

After reciting these words, blow out three breaths, imagining the energy of these words flowing through your breath into the ether, to your ancestors and any beings harmed by them, through all time and space.

THE N-WORD

⋆ ⋆ ⋆

A core component of historical white cowardice is using language to strip the dignity from people of color—not just Black people but all people of color. Whether it is the use of the N-word or other harmful words used to diminish the humanity of others, language has incredible power to do harm.

The power of language to harm the psyche of others is something I knew well as a child. I was rarely called by my name growing up; instead, I was given unwanted nicknames by my father, stepmother, brother, and others who wanted to continue making me feel less than human. These names demeaned me, and I do not wish to repeat them. They were used often as ways of stripping away my identity.

Strangely, growing up, I didn't use the N-word, even though I lived in a very racist household. This was because of my mother, who was externally very liberal in her politics; however, that didn't translate to authentic compassion and she was still very racist underneath. She would praise Dr. Martin Luther King Jr., and yet sometimes refer to anyone who was not white as "those people." But she told me not to use the N-word, and I tried to live accordingly.

But still something inside me was diseased. I mention this because I think it is worth examining this externalized liberal expression which tries to appear not racist, yet often is very racist deep down. Language in itself can be so powerful that one can internalize a harmful word and never use it but still be causing psychic damage to others. That was the case with me for many years.

In third grade I got into a fight because I stood up for a Black kid in our class named Clifford who was being taunted on the playground with the N-word by a white kid named Hank. I remember being called with Clifford and Hank to the principal's office. "What were you all fighting about?" our principal, Mr. Romero, asked. I told him that Hank kept calling Clifford the N-word. Mr. Romero released me and Clifford from his office, and went on to paddle Hank, which was a common punishment at the time. I was so proud of myself, but I would not say I was ever really friends with Clifford. I am glad I stood up for him, but I had my own inner racist demon inside, one I would not discover for many years.

It wasn't until my early twenties, when I began to work to heal my issues around childhood sexual abuse that I discovered the ugliness inside me regarding race. In therapy, I was learning the difference between thoughts and feelings, something I hadn't really understood before then, and learning how to separate the feelings were authentically my own from those I had simply taken on like emotional attire from my parents and immediate family. Though I didn't use the N-word, at times I would feel the energy of it enter into my emotions. I am ashamed to say this, but I admit it with hope that it helps heal our culture.

As I tracked the origin of this hatred that was inside of me, I was able to see that it was coming from encounters I'd had years before with my father's relatives and friends. It was as if a seed of ugliness had contaminated me and been planted in my brain and heart. The inner work I did on myself first involved acknowledging these feelings before I could transform them. For instance, why did I cross the street when seeing a Black man walking on the same sidewalk as me? I had never been attacked by a Black man, whereas I had been punched up in fights with other white people, regardless of gender. One white employee of my father had even attacked my older brother with a hatchet once, burying the blade of it into my brother's arm. So why didn't I cross the street when white men were coming toward me on the sidewalk? Why did I do this only with Black men?

This process went on over several years, and the more I wrestled with it, the more I began to see my own conditioning, my own insanity, and to understand that I was paranoid of being harmed by a Black man, when in fact I had witnessed my white family members kill an innocent Black man. The people worth fearing were my own family members, my own race, rather than people who had different colored skin than mine. If anything, based on historical fact, Black people should be afraid of my family, and by association, me, not the other way around.

I began to mix with Black culture for the first time while living in Oakland, California, in 1991. I was a poet and aspiring writer in the San Francisco Bay Area, and I was between seasonal jobs in outdoor education. I had just three hundred dollars to my name, and I rented a cheap room in someone's home by the week. I was lucky to be hired at a fast-food restaurant in Oakland near Lake Merritt called Kwik Way. The restaurant had an almost all-Black staff, and a majority Black clientele. There were two white people who worked there: me and a woman in her forties who was a former taxi driver on parole for shooting a man in the leg when he avoided paying his fare. As I worked there, over a period of five months, the distrust inside me and the paranoia finally dissolved.

My in-person experience invalidated all the hateful energetic imprints I had absorbed growing up with people who were filled with racist thoughts.

One night the manager, a Black woman named Mae, asked me to go work at a Kwik Way location in a rough neighborhood in East Oakland.

"You got money for a taxi?" she asked me.

"No," I said.

"Take this," she said, handing me a twenty-dollar bill. "I want you to make it home safe after your shift."

I thanked her and took the bus to the other Kwik Way location, where I worked until 1:00 a.m. During that shift I had several milkshakes thrown vigorously at me by young Black teenagers outside, but the thick, bulletproof window easily protected me. I think they bought the milkshakes simply with the intent of lobbing them towards me and the others working behind the window. There was a round, rotating bulletproof window through which we handed out the orders, unlike the Kwik Way at Lake Merritt, where you could place the meal directly into a customer's hands.

It would have been easy to take a taxi home that night, but after my shift I walked outside instead. I sat on a wooden bench by the bus stop, about half a block across the street, simply dismissing the fear every time it tried to rise up inside me. I paid attention to my breathing and the flickering street lights nearby, not the noise in my head. I kept reminding myself I had nothing to fear.

On the bus home, I tried to put things into perspective. I had been raped, beaten, and abused by my very white family. So, why did I need to be afraid riding home, even if this was a rough neighborhood? I could breathe through the fear. I could imagine myself safe and know these were just teenage kids being wild, not much different than I had been in my teenage years. I had done a lot of wild, crazy shit as a teenager, things that could have gotten me or others killed, so why should I be so afraid of these milkshake-tossing teens just because of their color? If they were white kids, would I be taking a taxi home? No, I wouldn't.

And so I had dismissed Mae's advice, feeling my own internal social experiment was more important, knowing I would be fine. I rode home that night feeling safer than I had in school, when I had ridden on all-white buses where jocks and aspiring cheerleaders patted gum into my hair to humiliate me. I was a dandruff-laden, shame-ridden, sexually abused kid at the time, and they rightly sensed that I had no self-esteem. But that night in Oakland, when I took the bus home from Kwik Way, I learned something about myself and defeated a demon that had been lurking inside me for years. And I gave Mae her twenty-dollar bill back the next morning,

That period at Kwik Way changed me forever. It wasn't necessarily fun much of the time. Several of those months took place during the Persian Gulf War, and many of the customers were angry at me for being the lone white man. Every day, random customers asked me if I supported the war, which I did not. "Are you for this war or against it?" they'd say. I could feel their anger at me for being white and not in the military.

"It's our boys fighting this war, you know," they'd tell me. "Our blood for their oil. It's your people getting richer, not us."

I would leave work feeling a kind of psychic film covering me when I went home, like a blanket of other people's hatred and anger aimed at me because of my color. I didn't like it, but at the same time I kept asking myself if this was what it was like for Black people most of the time, to feel anger and hate being dumped on them constantly from society in general. It made me think about the psychic game I had played in my mind so many times while I was crossing the street just because a Black man was in my path.

Did he feel it when I did that? I wondered. *Did he feel my distrust, my canceling of his humanity?* Of course, he did. *Does he experience it daily?* Of course, he does. *Is what he's experiencing like having a layer of pain in the aura?* Yes, absolutely.

I remember what it did to me to be taunted as a child and to have my own family repeatedly call me a name that was intended to demean me. It was hell experiencing that for the first twenty years of my life. I cannot imagine having to deal with that for a lifetime, or for that same pain to accrue over many, many generations like some hateful interest rate as it has with the N-word— which has stripped people of their dignity for five hundred years—and the collective psychic pain that goes with it. This is why we cannot say that word, and why we are obligated to strip the energy of that word from our consciousness through all time and space.

CHAPTER 4

TRANSFORMING THE RACIAL HATRED BEHIND THE N-WORD (AND OTHER RACIAL SLURS)

★ ★ ✖

Many years ago, while traveling with my brother and my maternal grandparents to Houston, Texas, where my mother's side of the family came from, my brother and I were horrified at how my grandparents spoke about Black people among their old friends. Phrases like "Those people don't know their place" came from the same lips that told me never to use the N-word. This split reality also existed in my mother. She only had friends who were white, and seemed uncomfortable around people who were Black, even though she projected an external facade of wanting to be for Civil Rights and racial equality. While spending several years in therapy, focusing on having been sexually abused by several family members, I came to see how I had also been conditioned emotionally by my family, and how my points of view on everything from art to music to politics and race were all part of the same emotional continuum—one that was designed to support a framework of lies. I began to see that I too had my own discomfort with people who were not white, and that this internal emotional landscape was something I had inherited rather than created.

Racism expresses itself not only systemically but also at the individual level as mental/emotional disease that has been created in the greater laboratory of our history. As a white man in a family that on my mother's side seemed quite liberal, I still learned to distrust and be uncomfortable around people who were not white. I grew up in New Mexico, and many of my family members would get irate whenever the people whose families had lived there for over three hundred years—much longer than mine—spoke in public the language with which they were raised, which was Spanish. Why did that spark discomfort for my family? Why did it create rage in my family—a rage I embodied until I began to question and dissolve my inner racism? My family didn't use racial slurs openly, and yet the energy that is behind those slurs existed quite openly in my family, and in me, I am ashamed to say.

So, how did I transform the negative energy inside me? It began as part of a greater self-inquiry process, involving simply asking myself continually how I was feeling. This was an acting technique developed by the method acting teacher Eric Morris, with whom I studied for a short time. Eric called it "taking personal inventory." I would ask myself the question out loud: "How do I feel?" Then I would respond in the moment by expressing my feelings aloud. This technique showed me that my thoughts and emotions were not the same, and that feelings can swiftly change from one moment to the next if we are open to their uninhibited flow. I learned that even though I *thought* I was an open-minded liberal in favor of racial equality for all, underneath that thought was an emotion of discomfort toward people of color that was not based on anything real, but rather on the conditioning I had learned from my family.

The more I began to see this and bring the absurdity of it into my consciousness, the more I was able to let go of my race-based anger and prejudice. I now embrace having friendships with Black people as well as with other people of color. And when I hear people speak a language other than English in public, I no longer feel triggered by it; I only feel ashamed that at one time in my life I did. And though I wish I spoke more languages than I do, it is musically and sensorially pleasant to my ears when I hear people speaking a foreign language, and I do not know the underlying meaning of what is being said. Focusing on the sounds and not the meaning makes the sounds become more pronounced and musical to my ears. My mind drifts into a place of wonder and magic, rather than harboring some inherited anger which never made any sense to begin with—an anger I took on like other forms of emotional attire from my dysfunctional family.

★   ★   ★

THREE-WEEK JOURNALING EXERCISE

The deep work of transforming internal racial hatred is a process, and not something that can be resolved overnight. But if you commit to the process, it will eventually liberate you.

Begin by getting a journal dedicated to this work. Make a daily practice of writing your observations about race in the journal, noting situations in which you felt triggered about an issue related to race. Do not judge your observations or try to be politically correct because that will lead to you steering your language to create an impression intended for others, rather than being authentic with yourself. For the first week, simply write down observations as they feel authentic to you.

In the second week, add another layer to your observations. If you are writing about feeling afraid of someone as you walk down the street because of their race or color, write why. It may be that in the answer to the why, you notice this was something you were taught by your parents, or maybe learned through images of how certain races are portrayed in the media. Whatever your answer is as to why, be authentic to it. Write the answer down and keep asking yourself if this rationale behind your feeling is real and true. There may be some instances in which you have had an authentically negative experience with someone from another race, and that has translated into a filter through which you now see all members of that race. Do not be ashamed of those experiences; simply write them down and continue to sift through them as if you are engaged in the archeology of your own consciousness—because, in fact, you are.

For week three, take your journal writing to an even deeper level. Get some pastels in various colors, or even just some crayons. Continue writing down your observations each day as before. Also, reread your entries from the second week, and if there are instances that still hold an emotional charge or have caused you to feel prejudice towards another race, investigate these incidents further by drawing your feelings about them. Do this in three scenes. For the first scene, simply allow your feelings about that event to be expressed on the page. If it is a situation that made you angry, you might use red tornados or some similar image to express that anger. Just let your hands pick the colors and express the feelings through them without premeditating or analyzing it.

Once you have expressed an emotion on paper, ask yourself how you wish things were, regarding the experience that triggered it. How would it look in the best of all possible worlds? Now let your hands again choose the pastels or crayons and create your own images, letting the process be organic and without premeditation. Once the images have been created, take a good look at them. How do you feel when looking at these images?

Compare these images to those of the previous drawing. Notice how you feel when you look at the first drawing, and how you feel when you look at the second drawing. Now do a third drawing of what you need to change within yourself to create that desired best-of-all-possible-worlds outcome. Again, let your hand grab the pastels or crayons to doodle and dance on the page without premeditating. Once your hand has finished the drawing, look at it. Ask yourself if there are practical baby steps you can take in your own life to begin the journey of inner change. Write down these steps and commit to taking action on them.

Commit to making this three-week cycle an ongoing process that repeats itself. Dig deep within your own consciousness through your journal and exercises. Remember that you are unique, and though racism is systemic, we each have our own history and emotional triggers when it comes to racist behavior. The more you engage in this process, the more you can begin to unwind prejudices, become free from internalized hatred, and create a better world around you by bringing your better self to it.

CHAPTER 5

THE BULLSHIT RULES ("BRULES") OF RACISM

★ ✦ ✹

I love the work of Vishen Lakhiani, the founder and CEO of the personal growth company Mindvalley, creator of the Soulvana meditation app. I am a member of Soulvana's energy healing faculty, and it is through that connection that I've come to learn about Vishen's important work. In his book *The Code of the Extraordinary Mind*, Vishen explores a concept of what he calls "brules," which is short for "bullshit rules." He explains that we are taught these brules by our parents, teachers, and society as a whole; many of us often rarely even question these brules and simply assume they are true.

My experience as a child in a racist household showed me that racism is nothing more than a collection of brules, and the path to freedom for anyone who grows up in a racist culture requires a moral obligation to challenge these brules, first internally and then in the public sphere. The racist brules that I was exposed to while growing up were that some races are less intelligent than other races, some are less motivated, some are less caring, and most horrendous of all, that the lives of the people of some races hold little or no value. Essentially, when my father's friend Clyde bragged about killing a young Black boy, his actions were essentially telling me and everyone around me that Black Lives Don't Matter. That racist brule was the basis for enslaving millions of people for hundreds of years.

Other common racist brules are in the form of images. The Confederate flag, an emblem for promoting white supremacy, is a racist brule that exists as a symbol displayed on bumper stickers, T-shirts, or flags. This symbol implies that there is something romantic about the Old South, some idealized concept of Dixieland and the "rebel"—but, in fact, the Old South was a human factory farm, where human beings of color were owned, beaten, raped, and deprived of their basic dignity as human beings.

Racist brules do not have to be in the form of language; they can also be images, actions, things we do, or things we avoid seeing. Another racist brule is that it's okay to be silent about issues of racial disparity. As a white person, I have come to be very aware simultaneously of the subtle ways in which I and others are at times encouraged to be silent and not speak up about race, and of how easy it would be for me to keep quiet if it were not for my conscience. Truth be told, I am saddened by the number of times I've posted on social media about issues related to race and received negative comments from members of the Reiki community, a community I hold dear to my heart. These comments are not widespread, but they are enough to remind me that even in the world of energy healing, racism can exist and be reinforced through the idea that we should all just be peaceful and not discuss protests, social justice, or similar themes.

★ ✦ ✖

HOW TO CHALLENGE YOUR RACIST BRULES

The way to begin challenging these racist brules is to become fully aware of which ones may have influenced you while you were growing up and may even still be influencing you today. To explore this, take out your notebook and methodically list any racist brules to which you may have been exposed while growing up, whether you actually believed those brules or not.

Next, write down in detail how you first learned or were exposed to each brule. Was it from a teacher, relative, textbook, television show, or friend? Track who in your life was promoting these racist brules. Were they promoted through words, actions, images?

The purpose of this exercise is to bring to your awareness the mechanisms of your social conditioning around race. What you may find is that once you begin this process, it will go deeper than you think. You will begin to notice how the landscape of your own consciousness was and is influenced directly and indirectly by others. We exist in an ecosystem of consciousness, and we are vulnerable to the effects of what other people say and do. Often, we do not immediately realize how an unkind word repeated over and over can tear into the roots of our soul, or how an image witnessed repeatedly can unconsciously create expectations or fears that may have absolutely no basis in reality.

By bringing these bullshit racist rules into the light, we strip them of their power over us. We name them for what they are, rather than let their toxins leak into us. The populace of ancient Rome didn't object to the fact that their water pipes were made of lead. They had no information to indicate that lead would be harmful to their brains. Nevertheless, their minds were exposed to the lead toxins in their water. Similarly, there are toxins in our cultural ecosystem that many of us do not question, nor even see as toxins.

By actively searching for the racist brules in our own lives, we can see them for what they are and release their influence on our consciousness, both individually and collectively.

CHAPTER 6

HEALING GRIEF

n spring 1999 I began to shift the focus of my graduate studies
to include healing my trauma related to having witnessed a race-
based murder as a child. One exercise I did was for a graduate-level
art class, when I created a painting to embody and express the grief
I felt over witnessing this murder.

My process for the painting began with writing to the spirit of
the Black man I had watched being killed many decades ago. I
wrote several long letters expressing the pain I felt for his death
and my guilt for being a member of the family who murdered him.
I then ritually burned the letters, intending that my words would be
sent to the man's spirit through the flames.

That very healing act was based on a magical ritual I had been
taught many years before, involving writing a letter to the higher
self of another person and then burning it. This technique has been
very effective for me in situations where I could not—or would
not—contact the person face-to-face, including those who had sexually abused me as a child, and has always brought healing to me.
For this ritual, I saved the ashes of the letter in a mason jar.

Next, I bought a large canvas, about six feet long and three feet wide, on which I could easily portray a life-sized adult human fig-ure of average proportions. My drawing abilities are not very good, but my purpose was not to be realistic but rather to express my grief fully and visually. I laid the blank canvas on the floor of my studio apartment and sat looking at it, wondering how to go about making an image to convey my grief. Then, slowly and deliberately, I dipped my fingers into the jar and began smearing the ashes on the canvas, creating the outline of a human body. I then focused on the face, giving the mouth a wailing expression and drawing tearful eyes, and with each touch of my fingers, the canvas felt more and more like a living embodiment of my grief regarding this man's murder. When the drawing felt complete, I took the canvas outdoors and sprayed it with a sealant to bind the ashes.

At San Francisco State University, where I attended graduate school, I displayed the canvas in the classroom, with a short art-ist's statement indicating my process. I wrote that the drawing was intended to capture my grief over witnessing a race-based murder when I was a child. I was not able at that point to indicate that the crime had been committed by my family members, though for my final thesis performance six months later, I would find the courage to be that honest, and the process of going public with my pain and grief was very healing for me.

This ritual exercise can be used to bring about healing for your own racial grief. You don't need to have witnessed a murder to need healing. Simply by being part of contemporary culture, you are also part of a collective mindset that has allowed great harm to occur to indigenous people and people of color over many centuries around the globe. The purpose of transforming this grief is to honor it and deepen into the process of uncovering our collective shadow. As long as we continue to deny that shadow and short-circuit our grief, we also short-circuit our empathy for those who have been harmed by racial crimes and racial bias. The collective mentality of white cowardice behavior requires that we remain emotionally inept. To transform our culture, we must face the pain, grief, and sorrow caused by these crimes and biases.

★   ★   ★

To transform your personal grief around racism, begin with the instance that has the biggest emotional charge. Think of the event and the person (or people) to whom you want to express your grief. If you find it too difficult to start with a personal event, draw upon an event in our collective history such as the assassination of Dr. Martin Luther King Jr., the 1921 Tulsa Race Massacre, the recent deaths of Black men and women at the hands of police, or myriad other crimes. (And if you still cannot think of who to address, I suggest writing to the spirit of one of George Washington's slaves whose teeth were extracted to create the president's dentures. Contrary to the myth, Washington's dentures, which are on display in the museum at his Mount Vernon estate, contained slave teeth, not wood.)

★   ★   ★

EXPRESSING YOUR GRIEF THROUGH RITUAL ART

Even if you are an atheist and do not believe in spirits or higher selves, try this exercise for the emotional release that will happen in the process.

Once you have identified a racial injustice event, choose a specific person who was harmed during it. If you don't know the person's name, research it online. Being willing to do some research also invests you more in knowing the history of racial injustice. Once you have the name of a person who was harmed by racial injustice (and it does not have to be a murder, as happened in my case), then write a letter to that person's spirit if they are deceased or to their higher self if they are still alive. Think deeply about the grief you are trying to express and be deliberate about expressing it.

Start by imagining the person standing in front of you. In this process, once you write the letter and burn it, you will be sending the contents of your letter to their spirit or higher self.

Begin your letter as a freewrite, letting your pen flow across the page as your emotions and thoughts spill forth. I recommend setting a timer, which will help you write faster and unedited. Set the timer initially for five minutes. If your letter feels incomplete after that time, you can spend more time. I find that if I do not set a time limit, I sometimes meander verbally and end up saying nothing at all; but setting a time limit makes me more direct and more honest.

Know too that this is your first attempt. It is your own emotional expression. I recommend repeating the process more than once, so do not feel it needs to be perfect the first time.

Once you have finished the letter, ceremonially burn it in a safe place—a fireplace, an outdoor fire pit, or even a used metal pot at a park. Just make sure you are being safe and not setting a fire inside or outside your home or in the wilderness.

As the letter burns, visualize its contents being sent on the higher planes of reality to the recipient's spirit or living higher self. Let the power of the flame release your energies. Once the letter is burned, allow the paper to cool before collecting the ashes.

You can repeat this letter-writing process numerous times. The letters can either be to the same person of a deeply charged event or to a different person each time you write. The choice is yours; simply use this technique to explore your grief, honor the person (or people) harmed, and delve deeper into transforming your own psyche. After each letter is written, burn it ceremonially as you did with the first letter, and collect the ashes.

Continue the letter-writing process until you have a mason jar full of ashes. This process might take a few hours, a few days, or even a few weeks. Once you have the mason jar of ashes, get yourself a sketchpad. (Most people will not have the opportunity to display a large canvas as I did, so a sketchpad can be more practical.)

Practice drawing just the face of your own grief in the sketchpad, using your fingers to personalize the experience. Really allow yourself to feel the emotions as they come forth—through your fingers, into the ashes, and onto the paper. Give yourself permission to draw more than one face of grief, allowing yourself to know that not all grief is the same.

Once you have a collection of faces of grief, pick at least one of them and display it somewhere it can be seen publicly, perhaps at a bulletin board in a coffeehouse, community center, health food store, or bus stop. One project I did in college involved posting art in bathroom stalls. I found that this method of displaying my art ensured me one captive audience member at a time, at least until the work got torn down by a janitor. I found it remarkable that the janitors at San Francisco State University would leave up misogynistic graffiti but swiftly tear down my small, harmless art projects that brought attention to social issues such as child abuse.

Know that you, too, will meet resistance. Your works of art will be disparaged, torn down, and get comments written on them. But the purpose of this project is to unveil the feelings behind your art. Nowadays, you don't need to resort to bathroom stalls or bulletin boards to get your art seen—you can simply post it on Instagram.

Each drawing that you do will uncover deeper layers of your grief. You needn't worry that you will be overwhelmed or destroyed by this grief, but you may—and hopefully will—experience a shift in your identity and begin to feel less affiliation with the white cowardice lies that our culture has taught you about race. And by starting to connect with your own grief, you will be able to begin a journey not only toward empathizing with those who have suffered great atrocities from our culture, but also toward becoming emotionally free and moving forward toward your own liberation.

CHAPTER 7

THE POWER OF WITNESSING

AND EXPRESSING EMPATHY

★　★　✦

Recognizing the trauma others have experienced is essential in transforming our society as well as making us more compassionate in our interactions. This is especially true when it comes to issues of racial trauma. In our culture, there can be an unhealthy "get over it" mentality, which is a phrase I have heard far too many times in conversations about race, especially when white people say things like, "Slavery ended over a hundred and fifty years ago, time to get over it." It's true that slavery in the United States legally ended over a century and a half ago, but that was followed by a period of white terrorism, manifesting in the South's Jim Crow laws, segregation, and bank policies like red lining that made it more difficult for people of color to buy a home, not to mention mob lynchings and the hateful activities of the Ku Klux Klan and other groups. By no means does society as a whole treat people of color with the same level of dignity as most white people are treated. And even if society did that, it would still would not undo the generational trauma inflicted upon Black and brown people, to which many white people still choose to remain blind.

As a young boy, in spite of my racist environment, I would still yearn for the day to come when it would be commonplace for white people to apologize to people of color for crimes like slavery as an act of human decency, as simple and common as saying hello to others on the street. Apologizing for crimes like slavery may seem impractical or naïve to some, but there needs to be some act of witnessing and honoring the pain of other races, especially Blacks and Native Americans who faced cultural atrocities on a grand scale.

The best way to begin this journey is to begin creating a baseline of empathy with those who have been the victims of racial injustice for centuries, to be a witness and hold a space in your heart for their pain, and to verbally acknowledge this to them with a sincere heart whenever circumstances offer you the opportunity to do so.

The practice I described in the previous chapter, writing a letter to someone's spirit or higher self and then burning it in a ceremonial way, can be adapted to help you begin witnessing and expressing empathy. Remember, our society is in many ways similar to a family in which incest and abuse have occurred, but the very act of talking about the abuse is taboo. Talking about slavery on an emotional or spiritual level is often taboo in this country. We would be a far healthier nation if open conversations about race were commonplace, and if our conversations did not simply remain in the political or intellectual realm but also offered tears and remorse for the unjust conditions in which people of color have lived for hundreds of years—conditions that in fact still exist today.

★ ★ ★

THE LETTER OF EMPATHY

This ritual is intended to begin heartfelt communication about race between you and a person of color who is alive. In this case, you will send a letter first to the living person's higher self, as way of gently easing into the difficult process so many people completely avoid. The end goal is that this first draft eventually becomes an actual letter that you can mail or, better yet, use for the basis of an in-person conversation.

Begin by writing the letter, expressing your empathy, and bearing witness to the person's suffering. Here is an example you can adapt and personalize:

Dear _____,

I want to release the pain and suffering my race has caused to you and your ancestors. I want to acknowledge this publicly, and I am also scared of how to do that.

Emotions around doing this have been pent up in me during this short lifetime as well as inherited through generations, and this generational wall of silence is hard to begin to break down. This letter is not meant to be the end, but the beginning—a way of lighting the way for my heart to be empathetic, not just in secret, but also in public.

I apologize to you for what my race did to yours: the enslavement, the rapes, the murders, the stealing of human beings, the stealing of land, the stealing of dignity, the genocide, and the ocean of tears that have turned into ice in a way that makes it almost impossible to have an authentic emotionally sincere conversation about this topic. But I want to try, and I want you to know this. I want you to feel this, to be touched on the psychic level when I burn this letter. May the flames of this letter begin to melt that ice as soon as these words are set on fire. May we burn down the legacies of hatred, of fear, and of white terror. May we burn these legacies together. And may all beings of love and kindness, on all levels, support this work.

In witness to you and all you have endured,
Sincerely,

★　✦　✹

Feel free to adapt this language and personalize it. Once your letter is written, ceremonially burn it as you did the letters you wrote for similar rituals in the previous chapters.

Repeat this exercise often until the letter becomes one you can put in the mail, send as an email, or, best of all, use as the basis of a live conversation between the two of you.

CHAPTER 8

RAISING YOUR VOICE,
IN MORE WAYS THAN ONE

★ ✦ ✹

White silence on the issue of racism is a big reason why it has been so hard to create long and lasting change. The inability of whole segments of the population to speak about police brutality when this brutality includes murder, sometimes even caught on film, is insane. You can help end that silence by bringing your voice to protests and by speaking to family and friends about these issues and related ones like the mass incarceration of Blacks.

Know that the power of your voice creates change each time you use it. That power, however, is more than just communicating your position to others. The sound of the human voice can also bring healing to the body and psyche. Sound-healing techniques have been helpful for many in their own healing process.

While working at Omega Institute, I have been exposed to a wide variety of healing modalities and I have seen that the sound-healing technique of toning is one of the simplest and most effective healing processes available. Toning is the process of making sounds to clear energy from your energy field and the very cells of your body.

It can also be used to clear the energy cords between you and others and to shift your consciousness by releasing unwanted thought patterns, clearing blocked emotions, and undoing energetic obstacles to your authentic self.

While toning is a very easy alternative therapy for clearing yourself on many levels, for our purposes, toning is focused on the mental and emotional layers of the aura to clear our racist-energy imprints and any racist conditioning that we may have taken on unconsciously, as well as to release racial trauma at the cellular level. Once you feel confident using toning on yourself, you can also use it to clear situations energetically at a distance. The most beautiful thing about toning is it requires no initiations, no intensive training. It is a technique anyone can use; all you need is to have the will.

★　✦　✹

TONING TO CLEAR RACIST IMPRINTS

First find a place where you can make some audible sound without being disturbed by others: your bedroom, your backyard, maybe even your garage. (Toning can also be practiced in a public or natural setting if you feel comfortable doing so.) You can sit or stand, whichever is comfortable for you; I personally prefer to sit for this exercise.

Begin by tuning in to your energy field and asking for a sound that will help you clear your energy field in general. Then simply make the first tone or sound which comes to mind. Usually it is a vowel sound, such as A, E, I, O, or U, but can also be a consonant sound, such as an M or R sound. The volume of the sound is not essential for this practice to work, so even if you don't have complete privacy and can only make the sound semi-audibly, it will still have an effect. Hold the sound for as long as you can on your first breath. Then, with your second breath, repeat that sound with the intention that it blasts away any energies in your field that are causing disharmony and imbalance. Repeat this several times for complete the initial clearing of your field. Toning can work very quickly, so even just a couple of minutes of this practice can clear energy at a very deep level.

Once you have completed the initial clearing, you can focus on clearing any patterns of racist imprints that may be in your energy field. You may not even be aware of these bits of energetic dust that cling to your energy body, but they can influence and filter how you think and feel similar to what happens when you walk into a room full of people who are very angry, and you feel their anger cover you like a coat of film. These racist bits of energetic dust can come from images you've seen in the media or from other people, and when this energetic dust accumulates over time, it can contribute to the development of an unconscious racial bias. Regularly practicing energy clearing allows you to bring it into your awareness and release it permanently.

Next, ask for a tone or sound to clear any racial bias you are holding on the conscious or subconscious level, and make the first sound that comes to you. As before, hold that sound for as long as you can with your first breath. It is not uncommon to cough, or even burp, if you are releasing something deep energetically, so if that happens to you, simply keep pressing forward as best as you can with your tone or sound. Now take a second breath and continue making the same sound out loud. Repeat this with as many breaths as you need to fully release the energy. You will likely sense the stuck energy being moved out, and you may also notice an area of your body suddenly feeling freer or opening as the old energy pattern is released. And even if you do not release the entire racist imprint pattern during the first session, you can use this technique again.

After you have finished the session, write about the experience in your journal, noting the feelings of openness in your energy field and your body. Also note any sensations that seem important and may hold information for you at a deeper level. These sensations may include a sense of tightness in an area of the body where more work still needs to be done. Simply notice these sensations and write down what you feel; even if you suspect that a sensation may just be in your imagination, write it down. Practice this technique on a regular basis, if not daily then at least weekly. By committing to clearing your energy field regularly, you are committing to rooting out your racial biases at a deep energetic level.

You may be surprised by how many old energy patterns supporting racist points of view you have buried in your energy field. These patterns often reflect old conditioning passed down to us from our ancestors and parents or things we picked up from our teachers, school, friends, the media, or experiences we had growing up. To work on releasing this old conditioning, do the toning as you did before, first as a general clearing; then choose someone in your past who was a source of racist conditioning. Ask for the sound that will clear you *in the past* from that person's conditioning. The idea of clearing something in the past might sound strange, but as an energy healer I have come to learn that energy healing is not bound by time and space. You cannot change the past, but you can transform the energetic signature of how past events are influencing the present. By sending healing to the past, you can change how the past influences you now and in the future. So, make that tone, literally aiming that energy with your mind toward yourself in that past situation. Intend that the toning you are sending now, in the present time, is shielding you and clearing you of the racist conditioning that occurred in the past at the moment in time in which it was created and reinforced. Intend that not only will this tone shield you, but that it will also clear away any energetic imprints that may have happened in the minutes or hours prior to this moment in time. Repeat this toning exercise several times, being very specific about who you are clearing yourself from. Making this process a routine practice will bring about a deep detox.

Another way you can use toning is to send healing out into the world. If you find there is racism in your home, school, or workplace, commit to a toning practice to help clear that issue wherever it has been occurring. For this practice, begin with tones to clear your own energy field at a general level. Once that is complete, ask for a sound to come to you to help clear the issue at the place you desire to heal. Go with the first sound that comes to you and let your voice embrace that sound at whatever level of volume you are comfortable with. Remember, even a semi-audible toning can still have an impact. Make the tone and notice the energy moving out from you toward the situation you want to clear of race issues. Again, this may be a personal place or even a government building where laws and policies are created, such as the White House or Capitol Hill, where a white supremacist insurgency incited by President Trump occurred on January 6, 2021. When clearing such powerful places, it is highly unlikely that one toning session will result in massive changes, but slowly, over time, piece by piece, the more we clear these institutions energetically—while also undertaking practical actions like voting, protesting, organizing, and writing letters to elected officials—the more likely those changes will occur at an accelerated rate.

Sound carries healing power. When a beautiful piece of music plays on the radio, it can change your mood. When I suffered a hematoma in an accident several years ago after falling down the stairs, part of my physical therapy involved ultrasound to break up the stuck fluid where my body was swollen and bruised. Scientists are now studying the healing power of sound, and monks and yogis have long chanted sacred mantras to bring healing.

You can use sound beyond simply toning, though it would require training I am not qualified to give. But if you already have that training, and can work with tuning forks, singing bowls, sacred mantras, or other ways to access the healing power of sound, I encourage you to use your existing training and incorporate it into the processes of clearing yourself and sending healing sound to situations to clear racism from homes, schools, workplaces, and government buildings. Such actions can have collective value over time, and we can envision toning, singing, and chanting our world into becoming a better place for everyone.

AFFIRMATIONS AND

LOFTY QUESTIONS

★ ✦ ✖

Many people find affirmations very helpful in their own personal transformation and healing processes. I began doing affirmations in 1986 after a car accident. For many months after the accident, I saw a chiropractor, and although she was working on helping heal the whiplash I had suffered, she could also detect my very low self-esteem. Although I never told my chiropractor that my being a sexual abuse survivor had brought about my low self-esteem, she sensed that I needed some easy-to-use tools to improve it. One day she led me over to a mirror in her office, told me to look into it, and instructed me in the very simple daily practice of tapping on my heart three times while repeating an affirmation aloud three times: "I deeply love and appreciate myself." As I stared into my own reflection, said those words, and tapped on my heart, I noticed that my eyes began to look different, as if an invisible river of love were flowing forth from them.

That was my first exposure to affirmations, and that single affirmation helped carry me through a long, difficult period while I first separated from my very toxic family. I spoke it aloud for many years and it got me through times of deep loneliness and despair. I no longer speak that affirmation daily, but I credit it with creating a sense of self-love during a critical time in my life.

Affirmations are widely used, and many people find them very effective. An affirmation is simply a positive statement designed to influence how you think, which works through repeating it over and over. When you make an affirmation part of your daily practice, the words of that affirmation infuse with your consciousness over time; the more you use the affirmation the more it becomes a part of who you are. As one who has worked at Omega Institute for over twenty years, where I was exposed to myriad alternative healing techniques, it has been apparent to me that many of these alternative healing techniques can also be adapted to heal the racist conditioning many of us carry inside of us. What follow here are some affirmations you can use to address racist conditioning inside of you. You may create your own affirmations as well. I typically say each one to myself three times. Try saying them in front of a mirror. If you would like, you may also tap on your heart while saying these aloud:

> *I honor the suffering of all races and cultures.*
> *I see the effect of my own racial bias and consciously release it.*
> *I am outspoken when I see racial injustice.*
> *I act for the benefit of all races, not just my own.*
> *I release any racist conditioning I have and transform it into love and acceptance.*
> *I deeply love and accept all races.*

These affirmations will not transform you overnight; they need to be repeated over and over to become fully engrained in your consciousness. But just as happened for me in my own healing journey, at a time when I could easily have turned to drugs or suicide to be released from my pain, affirmations can be a tool that is easy to access and can become a gateway to changing your consciousness with slow baby steps.

★ ✦ ✹

ASKING LOFTY QUESTIONS

Lofty questions are similar to affirmations, but some people find them more effective. I first learned of the concept of lofty questions from Christie Marie Sheldon through her personal growth videos on Mindvalley. These questions work by inviting our subconscious minds to fill in the blank of a question. For instance, someone who wants to create abundance in their lives might use a lofty question such as: *Why do I always have more abundance than I need in all areas of my life?* Asking why, rather than simply stating the desired goal, allows the subconscious mind to continue actively creating answers and real solutions for the question. This activation is why many people find lofty questions more effective than affirmations. Here are a few lofty questions you can ask to try to transform your own racist conditioning. I recommend posting them around your living space so you can see them and allow them to fully integrate into your consciousness.

Why do I always see my own racist conditioning and
transform it into love and light?

Why do I always speak truth to power when confronted
with the racist behavior of others?
Why do I always work on transforming myself for the
unity of all humankind?

I encourage you to write your own lofty questions, as well as to use affirmations. You may find that one technique appeals to you more than the other, but both can be effective for changing your consciousness and allowing you to detox from racist conditioning.

CHAPTER 10

HONORING THE SPACE

BETWEEN US

★ ★ ★

Energetically, there is a history we all carry. That history includes our direct ancestors, our collective actions as a race, the history of colonialism, and our own personal histories. It's all energetically with us everywhere we go. As a white man, I have intentionally worked to say hello to both my history and the history of the people with whom I interact. I may not know the other person's personal history, but I can and should honor the collective racial history that exists in the space between us. This goes deeper than identity politics—it is a humanization of a history that energetically exists in the space between any two people. By saying hello to the energy between us, I am honoring any collective suffering that may exist for someone else as person of color, and for the racial trauma that is there. This does not mean I am reducing someone to a racial stereotype or labeling someone because of their race. It is simply an energetic hello. I also do this with people I meet who are white.

What is an energetic hello? It is a hello that you say mentally to everything that is energetically present. If I am interacting with a person who is Black and had ancestors who were enslaved, I mentally say hello to the suffering of those ancestors and the generational trauma that exists. I simply say hello to it without going into a place of white guilt or pity for the other person. I am not whitewashing that person's history by overriding it, as many people do who say, "We are all one, all the same." On one level, yes, we are all one, and I strive to see human unity arising in us all. But at the same time, for that unity to be authentic there needs to be an honest honoring of any suffering carried in a person's energy field based on the lived history of their direct ancestors and their collective racial history. I am saying hello to the energetic imprints of oppression, any collective or ancestral racial resentment of oppression, and my own feelings, which may be the discomfort of being present with all that in my consciousness. For me to be fully authentic, I need to honor our collective history—both mine and the other person's.

★　★　★

THE MENTAL HELLO AND PINK ROSE

You can begin this process with anyone, regardless of race. Simply saying hello mentally, not only to who people are in the present moment, but also to their personal history (even if you don't know it), their ancestral history, their collective racial history, and if you want to engage the higher spiritual realms, their soul history, the timeline of their many lives, and the pain and wisdom that this timeline brings. You do not need to know these specific histories in order to energetically say hello to them. Here is a hypothetical example:

You are in an elevator with someone who is a Japanese American, perhaps a co-worker or maybe someone you barely know. You can simply say hello to them with your voice, to be polite. But in that same moment, imagine that you are saying hello to all of their energetic history in this life. Even if they have certain joys or traumas in their personal life of which you don't have any awareness, you can still mentally intend that you are saying hello to their life experience. You can then extend that to their family and ancestors. Maybe this person's ancestors were imprisoned in an internment camp during World War II, which was a collective racial trauma endured by Japanese Americans at that time. You can also say hello to that potential in the person's energy field as well as any trauma that their ancestors experienced and how that trauma affected later generations, which includes the person standing in the elevator with you. You don't need to know details of what happened; by saying a mental hello to the person and their collective racial experience, you also begin to empathize more with that person. Even if you don't know all the specifics of their personal history, ancestry, and collective racial experience, the act of a mental hello is a way to acknowledge that a history is there—and one that is very different than your own. By doing this, you acknowledge the person's humanity. And in honoring their humanity, you actually come closer to the idea of unity, which is a worthy goal. However, that goal can only be met when we acknowledge the truth of each person's experience, including their own personal stories, the stories of their family and ancestors, and the greater collective story of their racial history.

I will give you a personal example of this. My wife is American, born in Queens, New York. Her parents emigrated from Bangladesh to the United States shortly before she was born. When we first dated, I didn't give much consideration to her racial history. She was simply someone I loved and adored. But over the years, as I got to know her family and worked on trying to heal racist thought patterns in myself, I began to say hello energetically to my wife and her family and her ancestors. I also say hello to the village in Bangladesh where her ancestors lived and to her parents' struggle in coming to the United States and forging a new life without the support of that village, and I honor the fierceness that living in a totally new culture requires. I see all of this in my son too—with my wife's racial history and my own blending together in his beautiful smile. I say hello energetically to my son's history too, because just seeing him as an American boy would deprive him of his cultural heritage.

Make a practice of energetically saying hello to each person you meet. If you need a visual prompt for this, imagine the hello as a pink rose emerging from your mind and extending toward the person and their family, their ancestors, and their entire race. Making saying hello energetically a regular practice in your life will not only improve how you relate to other people, regardless of race, but will also create more empathy and a deeper lens for you in how you relate to others, energetically and beyond.

CHAPTER 11

CULTURE LOSS

★ ✦ ✹

One of my primary mentors in this life was a shaman named Carolion. I met her in Yellow Springs, Ohio, where we worked at a summer camp together. She was the wisest and most impactful healer I have ever met. She was trained through Michael Harner's Institute for Shamanic Studies, and though she completed her master level training with Harner and his assistant Sandra Ingerman, Carolion was her own brand of shaman. She knew the techniques she had been taught, but also expanded upon them. She would often use a dowsing rod rather than a rattle and drum and talked to plants and animals as easily as she spoke with human beings, and the information she received from plants and animals often proved extremely accurate. I eventually hired her to work with the staff at Omega Institute when I managed the staff programs there. One thing Carolion often talked about in our staff healing sessions was the deep sorrow that exists in many of us due to culture loss.

Culture loss happened for many indigenous peoples when their lands were colonized, their religions destroyed and replaced, and their entire way of life violently uprooted. The level of abuse that indigenous cultures all around the planet have endured during the past five hundred years is immense. But culture loss can also affect white people. As people emigrated to the United States from other parts of the world, they often lost their cultural heritage and gave up their cultural identity. The concept of the great melting pot, though having some advantages in the arena of personal freedom, also led to many of us having no real connection to our heritage. My own ethnicity is a combination of French, Greek, German, Irish, Dutch, and Cherokee. Yet I have little if any real sense of connection on a deep level to any of those cultures. You could say that I am part of white American culture, but even that is an abstract created by Madison Avenue that has resulted in a culture of fast food and shopping malls and is devoid of many of the symbols and rituals which enrich our sense of community and sustain life.

Grieving culture loss at the personal level is part of the process of racial healing. For as long as we have no connection to our own authentic culture, how can we empathize with those cultures that have been violently smashed and decimated by the legacy of colonialism? Also, it is when we feel we have no authentic culture of our own that we often appropriate the cultures of others. Mourning our own culture loss individually is the start of that healing process, so we can also extend that empathy to others who are also experiencing culture loss.

There are many ways you can begin to acknowledge culture loss at the personal level, including reading books from and about your own heritage; researching your heritage online; listening to music from your heritage; and grieving the loss of your heritage, since connections to cultural heritage cannot always be fully restored. I am not suggesting that you have to accept and adopt every practice that was prevalent in the village of your ancestors, but to at least acknowledge them, you need to come to an awareness of their absence in your life. Use the practice of energetically sending out a pink rose, as described in the previous chapter, to your own cultural heritage. Although you don't need to know the names of the people in your genetic family tree, if you can access that information it may be beneficial on some level. (However, that information is not required for this practice to work, so delaying this practice because you don't have that information is not recommended.)

Start to create a practice of sending a pink rose to your cultural heritage by simply standing in front of a mirror and looking at your image. Imagine mentally sending a rose to yourself and see it going to each family member, then back through time to your ancestors, at least several generations back. See this rose also going to your cultural heritage's symbols—for instance, its music, dances, art, language, and traditions. If you are not conscious of what these are, simply hold your intention of sending this pink rose mentally through time to those cultural expressions. If your heritage includes more than one culture, you can send a pink rose individually to each of those cultures or else send roses to all simultaneously. I recommend trying both approaches and seeing which one feels best to you.

By at least saying hello to your own culture loss, you can begin to empathize more with the culture loss experienced by those who have had their entire cultures smashed and destroyed by the practices of colonialism over hundreds of years. As your empathy grows over time, increasing with your regular daily practice, a deeper healing unfolds in the way you think, feel, and act. We become more whole by grieving our own culture loss, and as more people experience this, we together become like neurons in a brain trying to heal from our collective history. Over time, these small efforts will change the racist matrix in which we live by changing the energy around us, which in turn changes the culture of our families, our workplaces, and eventually our society as a whole.

SHAPESHIFTING OUR CULTURE

INTO UNITY CONSCIOUSNESS

★   ✦   ✹

My good friend John Perkins, a *New York Times* bestselling author who became a shaman while living in the Amazon rainforest with the Shaur people in the late 1960s, often writes about shapeshifting the dream of what our society is. One of his teachings is about the ancient prophecy from indigenous tribes in the Amazon of the eagle and the condor. This prophesy says that at some point, human societies would divide into two paths: the path of the eagle, which features rational thinking, the masculine, and leads to the industrial world; and the path of the condor, which involves the heart, intuition, and the feminine. According to the prophecy, for five hundred years, the eagle societies would become very powerful and almost wipe out the societies of the condor. This did happen, starting in the 1490s with colonialism, the mass genocide of indigenous cultures in the Americas, the institution of slavery, and the embodiment of racism that still continues to this day. At the end of this five-hundred-year period, says the prophecy, there would be the opportunity for the eagle and the condor to soar together under the same sky, raising the consciousness of humanity to a higher level.

But this prophecy is only a potential, not a certainty. It is a potential that requires us to do the deeper work of shapeshifting our consciousness to heal the wrongs that have taken place over the past five hundred years and begin a new dream.

★　✦　✹

Shapeshifting our consciousness requires going beyond just our rational mind and embracing the intuitive feeling parts of ourselves. I believe that healing the racist aspects of our society must include facing the emotions which underly that cancerous aspect of our world. Yes, we need to change our policies and laws, but if that is all we do, there will still be an energetic imprint in all of us that will act out in certain ways at the macro level because it has not been dealt with inside each of us at the micro level.

The healing I have experienced through John Perkins's workshops at Omega Institute over the past two decades has been profound. Some of the energy-healing techniques I have developed, which are the subjects of most of my books, were greatly influenced by shamanic journeys that happened in John's classes. In one class, John took us through a technique called the "Tibetan Star Meditation," a powerful meditation he learned from Tibetan shamans for manifesting and bringing about powerful changes in your own life. During that class, I asked him if he thought it would be effective for people to use this technique for creating positive social change on a mass scale. John said yes, but that the visualization has to be something specific, not vague—something each person can relate to on a personal level.

I have adapted the Tibetan Star Meditation to focus on creating unity consciousness when it comes to race—a unity consciousness so powerful and pure that any racist thought patterns, emotions, or racist beliefs cannot exist within it.

★   ★   ★

THE TIBETAN STAR MEDITATION FOR RACIAL HEALING

The first step is to dream of yourself being accepting of people of all races and being freed from all social conditioning that creates racial bias. You may even want to imagine a beautiful rainbow-colored light emanating from each cell of your body to represent this complete and authentic acceptance of all races.

Now, close your eyes and picture a deep, dark void, where there is no light at all—a void from which all potential arises. When you can fully see this void in your mind's eye, allow a silver star to appear within the center. Project your goal of being completely accepting of all races and freed from all racial bias or prejudice into that star. See the silver star envelop and absorb your dream entirely.

Once you have witnessed the star absorbing your dream, visualize it coming into you through your third eye, which is located on your forehead between and slightly above your eyebrows. Now picture your mind as if it were lined with mirrors, reflecting and amplifying the dream splendidly in myriad directions inside your head, like the infinite reflections you see when holding two mirrors up to each other, but in this case, there are many mirrors reflecting in all directions.

Now see the star explode in your mind. But rather than being destroyed, the star is energized, becoming more powerful and radiant and integrating into your mind.

Watch it explode a second time, growing even more radiant and powerful and once again integrating into your mind.

Visualize a third explosion of the star, where it grows even larger, illuminating your consciousness on all levels and fully integrating into your mind.

Next, picture the star moving down into your heart, which is also lined inside with a multitude of mirrors. See the star explode inside your heart, again becoming energized and more powerful, and then integrating into your heart.

Witness the star exploding in your heart a second time, and see the mirrors reflecting this explosion's light in myriad directions inside your heart, then watch as this light is integrated.

Now, visualize one last time the star brilliantly exploding, its million pieces radiantly shining inside your heart, and then the light becoming fully absorbed and integrated. Intend and feel the complete fusion of the dream, the star, and your heart.

Now watch as this star, which has integrated with your heart and your dream, moves back up into your head and back out through your third eye, and returns to the dark void of pure potential.

Repeat this exercise several times per week if possible, being as specific as you can be in feeling, seeing, and sensing the energy each time.

The more you practice this ritual, the more you will shapeshift the old cultural dream of dominance and racism into a new dream of unity and equality, both within you and around you.

CHAPTER 13

FREEING THE BODY

FROM RACISM

✶   ✶   ✶

My journey as a healer has taught me that real healing must happen in the body. If it happens only in the mind, it can remain an interesting thought, but more often than not, that thought remains an unrealized illusion. Again, transforming my own racist programming has been deeply intertwined with healing from sexual abuse, since, to me, these patterns feel quite similar. By taking care of my body, reclaiming my body and healing areas of my body where shame, self-hatred and other painful emotions were buried, I have been able to free myself of the chains of my past abuse, and I have used similar techniques to recover from racism.

These three simple and easy techniques are an effective process of creative detoxing from the energy of racism and for clearing the toxic energy that lives inside our bodies. Try all three techniques or let yourself gravitate to the one which serves you the most. Commit to making one, two, or all three rituals a regular practice to unwind the racist energies inside your body and release them forever.

✦ ✦ ✦

RITUAL BATH TO CLEAR RACIAL BIAS

The first technique is to make a regular practice of taking a ritual cleansing bath. Make the bath ritual personal to you. I recommend lighting a candle and having it burn safely in close proximity to your bathtub, while also burning incense, since aromas have specific qualities for cleansing and releasing. Sage, frankincense, and sandalwood are a few types of incense that I recommend, but make sure whatever you use is pleasant to you, an aroma that you enjoy.

Add a few pinches of sea salt to the water, as saltwater has wonderful qualities for clearing the human energy field of negative energy imprints. (Epsom salt can also be used if sea salt is not available, but sea salt is best for this type of cleansing.) As you draw the bath, visualize the water originating from a cleansing temple (an actual one or an imagined one).

You can also hold the intention that the bar of soap you use to wash your body is also washing away any racial bias you have taken on consciously or unconsciously. Intend that you are washing away your ancestral fear of people who look different from you as well as prejudice; negative images from the media to which you have been exposed regarding other races; and all internalized forms of racism on any levels from each cell of your body, even the ones inside of you that the soap cannot touch. This ritual, when practiced regularly, will create change; the changes will take place slowly at first, but eventually, the more you engage the cleansing bath as a practice, the more it will yield results of personal transformation.

✹ ✹ ✹

FINDING SELF-AWARENESS THROUGH SELF-PORTRAITS

Another technique I recommend is creating a self-portrait that is intended to reveal who you are when it comes to issues of race. This does not need to be an artistic masterpiece, so even if you have little or no talent for drawing or painting, please do not let that get in the way of doing this. In my own healing path, I often have used doodles to represent me, and also found these doodles to be incredibly healing and revealing of where I held negative images in my own body.

If you heard a lot of racist language growing up, you can express that in the way you draw your ears, perhaps using colors or adapting the lines in the drawing to reflect that, in whatever way feels right to you. Maybe you always wanted to speak out about issues of race but felt inhibited or fearful to do so; in the drawing, you can reflect that in the way you draw your mouth. Give your imagination the freedom to reveal this in whatever way works for you—the self-portrait does not need to be a realistic impression like a photograph but is instead a metaphor image intended to bring your awareness deeper into your own recovery from racism. When drawing your eyes, perhaps you will include tears expressing grief or sadness related to issues around race. Or, if you spent most of your life refusing to see the racism openly, you could draw one or both eyes either fully or partly closed. Let your imagination have full freedom of expression, without worrying about creating a realistic image of your physical self, for this drawing is intended as an image of healing and transformation.

If you enjoyed doing the first drawing, make more. You can dedicate an entire drawing pad to these types of drawings, and even make them cartoonlike. The purpose is to investigate yourself and bring to light the places inside you where change is needed.

★   ✦   ✹

BURNING AWAY INTERNALIZED RACISM
WITH CANDLE MAGIC

The third technique I recommend is a candle meditation, which can be very effective and even magical once you give your energy fully to the process. It is an easy process too, as long as you have a safe place where you can sit quietly with a candle for approximately ten minutes without interruption.

When I do this, I prefer it be in a dark room, with the only light coming from the candle flame. Those who enjoy ritual may want to consecrate the intention of the candle by first holding it in both hands and saying aloud, "The purpose of this candle is to burn away racial bias and conditioning," and then blowing that intention onto the candle before you light it. (This is not required, however, but for some people, expressing the intention in a ritualistic manner helps deepen the effect.)

Once you light the candle, simply sit in a comfortable position several feet away from it. Stare into the flame, and intend that any racist energy in your body, including the energy of emotions or thoughts, conscious or unconscious, goes into the flame and is burned away and transformed into love and light. As you hold this intention, imagine that with each inhalation you are bringing the flame inside you; seeing it illuminate at the cellular level any hate, distrust, suspicion, or false judgement you have been holding; and transforming those energies into the pure healing light of love. With each exhalation, intend that the light flows back out from your breath as love to anyone you have harmed, intentionally or unintentionally. Continue this process for ten minutes. When you have completed the process, give thanks to the flame of the candle for the work it has done, and then gently blow the candle out. Repeat this process as a ritual several times per week.

CHAPTER 14

EMBRACING TONGLEN

★ ✦ ✹

Tonglen is the Buddhist mind-training practice of taking in the suffering of others while sending well-being to replace that suffering. This ancient Buddhist practice, which dates back to the eleventh century, traditionally involves first becoming mentally present. You can do this by sitting comfortably and paying attention to your breath until your mind becomes calm and neutral. Continue focusing on your breathing until your mind comes into the present moment, just having an awareness of each breath, one at a time. Once your mind feels calm and present, call into your mind someone who is suffering, and intend that as you breathe in, you are taking in their suffering. As you breathe out, intend that you are sending compassion and well-being to that person, and watch that energy moving out through your breath.

Put this book down and try Tonglen for a few minutes before continuing to read.

★ ✦ ✹

Once you have experienced practicing Tonglen the way it is commonly used, focus it on racial suffering. Again, bring your mind into a calm place by simply paying attention to your breath. Once you feel calm and peaceful, call into mind a person who has suffered the negative impacts of racism. It is best if you can personalize this by choosing someone you know. If, for some reason, you have difficulty bringing an individual person to mind, then intend you are doing this practice for a collective of people, for instance, all people of color who have experienced police brutality. When you have selected a person or group of people for whom you will practice Tonglen, take a breath and intend that you are breathing in their racial suffering, including any historical racial trauma they might be carrying or experiencing. When you exhale, imagine that you are sending them well-being, compassion, and kindness. Repeat this process for five minutes, allowing this meditation to unfold, and put this book down in the meantime until the practice is complete. As you progress with Tonglen over time, these periods of meditation can go longer and deeper.

Notice how you feel after this initial practice. Does it create more empathy for you with the person or group for whom you were doing this practice? Give yourself a minute or two to do nothing other than allow yourself to observe how you feel before moving on to the next step.

★　　✦　　✖

The next step in this process is to focus the healing on your own ancestral lineage, adapting the practice even further and focusing on releasing racial bias from your ancestral lineage and replacing it with compassion and kindness toward people of other races.

First, bring your mind into a calm and neutral state by paying attention to your breathing, counting and focusing on each individual breath until you feel calm and in the present moment. Next, focus on your ancestral lineage. If that is hard for you to imagine, choose one grandparent or all four grandparents and intend that they are representative of your entire ancestral lineage. Now breathe in any racial bias that is held in your ancestral lineage. Even though you cannot change your ancestors' actions, you can change the energetic signature of their lineage (which extends to you) and how it affects you in the present moment. As you exhale, imagine that racial bias being transformed through your breath, back through your ancestral lineage, into the energy of compassion and acceptance for all races.

Put this book down and perform this practice for five minutes or longer.

★ ⁕ ✖

Now that you have been introduced to the Buddhist practice of Tonglen and have learned how to focus it on racial healing, I recommend making Tonglen a daily practice, knowing that you may very well experience internal resistance when focusing it entirely on issues of race. If you do experience resistance, understand that it is part of your own racist conditioning trying to undermine this process. That makes it all the more important to commit to Tonglen on a daily basis; I advise including the practice in your daily scheule, whether you write it on a paper calendar or in a datebook or enter it into an electronic calendar. Make the commitment to bring this gentle yet powerful spiritual practice into your life.

CHAPTER 15

THE HEALING POWER

OF GRATITUDE

★ ✦ ✹

Gratitude rewires the brain. Scientific studies show this. Happiness researchers know this. If gratitude can rewire the brain for personal happiness, then why not use it to change social programming and conditioning on race? It was when I was exposed to other cultures and began to appreciate them that my own negative racial biases began to change into gratitude and appreciation.

★ ✦ ✹

EXPRESSING MULTICULTURAL GRATITUDE

Practice offering gratitude for individuals or cultural attributes beyond your own, even if it means starting small. Start with the phrase "I am grateful for _____," and then fill in the blank. Make it a practice to say the things for which you're grateful out loud, even if you can only speak in a semi-audible whisper. It might sound something like this:

- *I am grateful for the music of Richie Havens, especially his song "Freedom."*
- *I am grateful for the poetry of Aja Monet and the truth of her words.*
- *I am grateful for the wonderful Zuni pottery I used to see in the windows of shops in New Mexico when I was a child.*
- *I am grateful for Navajo fry bread, especially when it's covered in honey.*
- *I am grateful for the friendship of my friend Nikku.*
- *I am grateful for the gift of African drumming, and the way it brings me into an alpha state of consciousness so easily.*
- *I am grateful for those Mexican and South American immigrants who work in the fields under harsh and usually unfair conditions, harvesting the fruit and vegetables I eat each day.*
- *I am grateful for the beautiful colors of Indian and Bengali saris in the shop windows near Roosevelt Avenue in Queens, New York.*
- *I am grateful for the wonderful smiles of the Balinese people each time I visit Bali.*
- *I am grateful for the courage of women like bell hooks and Sojourner Truth, and how, even as a man, reading about them makes me feel like a better person.*
- *I am grateful for Vishen Lakhiani and the beautiful work he has done in the area of human transformation from his offices in Kula Lumpur, Malaysia, and Tallinn, Estonia.*
- *I am grateful to the Iroquois nation and their traditions, which were so important to the writing of the United States Constitution.*

- *I am grateful to the Ecuadorian shamans who did powerful healing work on me during a workshop in 2000 at Omega Institute.*
- *I am grateful for the amazing Indian dhal dishes my wife cooks, based on her mother's recipes.*
- *I am grateful for my Yoruba uncrossing magical veve and how it has helped me release much of the dark energy of my childhood traumatic experiences.*
- *I am grateful for the Hindu practice of Kirtan and singing Divine names.*
- *I am grateful for the wonder of Balinese art, especially the immaculate Balinese wood carvings, and the deep artistic culture of Bali.*
- *I am grateful for the Thai Yoga I techniques I learned in Pai, Thailand, from a native teacher named Tiger back in 2002.*
- *I am grateful for the amazing speeches of Dr. Martin Luther King and his commitment to justice for all people, especially the poor.*
- *I am grateful to the bright, poetic mind of Muhammed Ali, and the influence he had on me as a sports icon and cultural activist during my childhood.*

★ ★ ✖

This simple exercise in cultural gratitude is like a muscle, and the more you use it, the more it will grow and widen the lens of your own perceptions of appreciation. The more you rewire your brain to appreciate and be grateful for other cultures and individuals from those cultures, the more you can contribute to bringing the world together.

Make it a daily practice to name at least twenty things for which you are grateful in celebration of individuals or cultural attributes not from your own race. It may seem very forced or even awkward at first, but the more you lean into it as a daily practice, the more you will genuinely grow your appreciation of the diverse world in which we live and simultaneously rewire any unconscious resistance you have to embracing the many gifts offered to the world by cultures and races other than your own.

★　★　★

LETTERS OF GRATITUDE

You can also take this process even deeper by writing specific letters of gratitude to individuals, living or dead, expressing your gratitude. Again, the intent is for the letter to be to someone of another race, one that is typically marginalized or oppressed, to reverse the energetic flow from oppression to gratitude. Even if you feel you are not participating in that oppression or marginalization, do this practice anyway to help generate the energy of gratitude. That energy will be felt beyond you as an individual. If your letter is to someone who is alive, I recommend mailing or emailing it to the recipient if possible. If the letter is to someone who is dead, then I recommend either keeping it in a place that feels sacred to you, like an altar, or burning the letter in a safe manner, intending that the flames are transporting your words to the recipient in the spirit realm.

Here is a letter I wrote to the spirit of Muhammed Ali, who was an amazing boxer, activist, and poet.

Dear Muhammed Ali,

I am grateful for the life you lived and how deeply it touched me as a child growing up. I loved the magic of your poems, the short rhymes about other boxers, and how you would "float like a butterfly and sting like a bee." I am grateful for the brilliance of your mind, your wit, the courage you displayed standing up against the war in Vietnam as a conscientious objector to being drafted, even though it led to your being convicted of draft evasion by an all-white jury and losing your boxing title for several years. I am grateful for the strength you displayed taking your case to the Supreme Court, and winning, and I am grateful for the strength you displayed years later by continuing in a fight after your jaw had been broken by Ken Norton.

You were an icon to me, someone who was amazingly talented in sports but who also stood for something. I remember listening on the radio in my mother's car the night you knocked out George Foreman in "the Rumble in the Jungle," as you called it, that boxing match in Zaire where you regained your world heavyweight crown. I remember the anger I could see in my grandfather's eyes every time you were on television bantering with Howard Cosell, and how seeing my grandfather's anger warned me about so many others I would encounter who were like him, pretending to be so liberal while harboring racial hatred inside.

You taught me so much, even though I never met you, never saw you other than on the television screen. I am grateful for the wisdom of your life path, your setting an example by following the courage of your beliefs, and how you inspired not only Black boys and girls to aspire to something greater, to be the greatest. Please know you also inspired me, a young white boy who saw your humanity, the gift of your spirit, which helped my own spirit push forward through challenges I didn't know I would overcome, but did overcome, in many ways because of the light you showed me and millions of people all around the world.

I sometimes still watch you in old videos, where you talk about all the white images in this culture, and how everything good is portrayed as white and everything bad is portrayed as Black. You spoke to me then, and you speak to me now, and I am ever grateful for the deep magic of your life inspiring my life.

I honor you, and I express my gratitude to you now, burning these words and sending them forth to your spirit, so that you know that you taught me how to dance, to dodge the jabs life was sending me, and how to play possum with your rope-a-dope technique so I could survive during times of abuse and save my energy for when the time was right for me to come out fighting.

I send this message through time and space to wherever your spirit is now, in the realm of angels, passing into a new life, or maybe existing on higher dimensions of reality that I cannot begin to imagine. You gave me hope, laughter, and it gave me so much joy just to see you on television offering your rhymes like candy into the ears of a nation that would reject you in so many ways because of your color and your religion, and yet you pressed onward. I am ever so eternally grateful to you. May the light shine forth through the words in this letter into the heart of your soul.

With reverence and gratitude,
Brett Bevell

★　★　✖

The first few times I practiced these exercises of gratitude, focusing on appreciating attributes and individuals from races other than my own, I felt extremely tired afterward, as if there was some deep energetic resistance to me doing this practice. You may experience something similar, as the matrix of our collective social consciousness still erects barriers to this type of work. You must move beyond the psychic sludge to embrace this practice, but the rewards for doing so are immense and will make you aware of how deeply trapped in our own racial boxes many of us are—even those of us who consider ourselves very socially liberated and aware.

You may also feel this exercise is simply silly, or even stupid, which is simply another manifestation of that same resistance of which I speak. It will hurt no one to try this practice. Try either the twenty daily gratitude statements or writing a gratitude letter, focusing in either process on the gratitude you have for cultural attributes or individuals outside your own race, and extending that circle of gratitude outside the ethnocentric worldview.

CHAPTER 16

REIKI AND RACISM

★ ✦ ✳

Reiki is the world's most popular form of energy healing. The word *reiki* can be translated from Japanese as "universal life force energy," or "Divine life force energy," depending on how one translates the Japanese *kanji*. This unique and powerful form of energy healing works on the assumption that, through a sacred initiation performed by a Reiki master, anyone who is willing to be initiated can access this beautiful healing energy—an energy that has an intelligence to it and is programmed to be always working for the highest good. Reiki can be found as a form of palliative care in many of the world's more progressive hospitals. In fact, many nurses earn continuing education credits by taking classes in Reiki and learning how to use this healing gift on their patients. Millions of people around the globe have now experienced a Reiki session or have themselves been initiated as Reiki practitioners.

I first learned about Reiki in early 1993 after having a miserable experience at the New York University dental clinic, where a student was quite aggressive in pulling my decayed wisdom tooth. When I got home after that painful experience, my roommate Eben offered me a Reiki session.

I had never heard of Reiki before, as Eben had never talked about it. But once the session began, I immediately felt a connection to something much larger than him, larger than me, and most importantly, larger than the pain I was experiencing. This gentle form of energy healing allowed me to go into a place of deep surrender and grace, which eventually radically and positively changed my life forever. And though I have deeply immersed myself in a journey of self-healing for more than thirty years, it was when I became initiated into Reiki and opened up to the world of energy healing that my life truly began to transform in beautiful ways.

All lineages of Reiki can be traced back to a Japanese mystic named Mikao Usui, who lived from 1865 to 1926. Shortly before World War II, a Japanese American woman named Hawayo Takata, who had trained and become a Reiki master in Japan, brought Reiki to the United States, where she taught Reiki to the public and eventually initiated twenty-two Reiki masters. Reiki has been growing and flourishing exponentially ever since.

There are three levels of Reiki, as it is taught traditionally. In the first level, a Reiki master initiates the student, and the student is taught how to perform a Reiki session on themselves and on another person. Typically, the student is also taught some of Reiki's history and five precepts, which are the guiding principles for daily life as set forth by Mikao Usui. In the second level of Reiki, the student is once again initiated by a Reiki master, and this time the student learns how to access and use three sacred Reiki symbols: the first for increasing the focus and power of the energy; the second for bringing harmony and mental/emotional healing; and the third symbol for sending Reiki distantly across time and space. In the third level of Reiki, the student learns how to become a Reiki master through being initiated again and learning all the traditional

Reiki symbols and how to use them for initiating others into this powerful healing system.

Becoming a Reiki master also leads the student deeper into their own soul journey, and there are many aspects to this, far beyond the scope and focus of this book. However, there are important ways that Reiki can be used traditionally to bring healing to issues of racism at the personal level and beyond. Even if you are not trained in Reiki, this chapter will teach you about these traditional paths, and you will be able to implement that knowledge in the following chapter, which includes a Psychic Reiki initiation.

Reiki can have profound positive impact on a person who is working through their emotional issues, releasing negative mental patterns and unwanted behaviors at their core roots. I know this from experience, and I have seen this kind of transformation happen for many of my clients and students. As I have mentioned several times, it was while I was healing from my issues around sexual abuse that I noticed similarities between the patterns of dysfunction I saw in my own family around incest and abuse and larger patterns in society around issues of race. It was almost as if these patterns mirrored each other, which makes sense if you bring the issues of racism into the personal and emotional sphere, not just the sociopolitical sphere.

I was raped. Slaves were raped. I was beaten. Slaves were beaten. I was told to be silent. Slaves were beaten for speaking out and usually never to read. I am not comparing my suffering to the suffering of any slaves; what I am saying is that the systemic patterns of my family's dynamics of sexual abuse and the cultural dynamics of racism and slavery are quite similar. Therefore, since Reiki transformed my life by changing the way I felt about myself, others, and the world around me, why can't it also be used to bring that same level of healing to issues of racism? It can. As I have discovered personally, Reiki can be used to heal and transform racist mental and emotional conditioning.

Anyone who is empowered to the second level of Reiki can use the mental/emotional healing symbol for clearing racist thought patterns and emotions. People who have been at the receiving end of this hateful conditioning can also use Reiki for their own healing. This is not typically talked about in Reiki trainings, nor do most other alternative healing modalities typically shape their trainings to encompass issues of race. We have not yet dared to go there. But now is the time.

If you are trained at the second level of Reiki or higher, I recommend making it a daily practice to use the mental/emotional healing symbol to bring healing for your own racial suffering, as well as to heal and transform any racial bias and bring that racial bias into your conscious awareness. Even if you believe that you have no racial bias, simply try committing to a daily fifteen-minute session for a week. Then see for yourself what may begin to arise from the shadows of your mind to be healed and transformed.

If you have not attained the second level of Reiki training, in the next chapter you will learn to access a powerful aspect of Reiki, called Psychic Reiki, which can take this healing process to an even deeper level.

CHAPTER 17

PSYCHIC REIKI

EMPOWERMENT

★ ✦ ✖

Psychic Reiki is a term I coined for a technique of working with Reiki that is nontraditional and works directly with the Divine intelligence of the Reiki energy. It was revealed to me during a mystical experience I had traveling in Laos during the winter of 2007, while I was staying in Luang Prabang, the former Royal Capital. I was traveling alone and became incredibly ill for several days. All the guidebooks said it was best to avoid going to a hospital in Laos if at all possible due to their poor conditions. After a few days of doing nonstop energy healing on myself in my room at a small boutique hotel, I had an instantaneous recovery. My spleen, which had been swollen to about the size of a small grapefruit, now felt fine. The fever I'd had for days suddenly disappeared, and I was incredibly hungry, so I went to eat lunch at a small Indian restaurant nearby. I found a small table with white plastic chairs outside and sat down alone. As I waited for my food to arrive, suddenly, I felt this amazing presence from one of the empty chairs, and I knew immediately that it was the spirit of Mikao Usui, the person to whom all Reiki lineages can be traced back. From his spirit came a ball of white light, which entered into the area of my heart chakra at the center of my chest.

I didn't completely understand this experience immediately, as Mikao Usui's spirit and the ball of light vanished almost as suddenly as they had appeared. Yet, during the weeks afterward, I had numerous mystical experiences, often involving new information about Reiki, alternative Reiki symbols, and strange complex mathematical equations that made no sense to me but when I contemplated them gave me a euphoric sense of the eternal Divine presence within all things, in all of existence. I eventually became aware that in my heart chakra area, where I had received that ball of white light, there now existed in front of my heart an energetic crystal made of the light and energy of Reiki. This Reiki crystal was also able to send the energy of Reiki anywhere I wanted it to go, allowing me to bypass the traditional symbols and techniques by basically being in psychic communication with the intelligence of the energy itself.

I know how far-fetched this idea sounds, and yet it has proven very effective in healings and workshops, and I have now used or taught this technique to thousands of people all around the world. If it were not one of the most effective healing techniques I know, I would not share it here since I am fully aware that many readers will be skeptical of it, and it may then cast doubt on the entire contents of this book. For this reason, I have saved these teachings for the final third of this book, in hope that those who have gotten this far will continue forward and at least try the techniques I will share here shortly.

Psychic Reiki, just like traditional Reiki, requires an initiation. I like to think of it like a software download into your energy system that allows you to access the energy of Reiki. This energetic software will change your life by changing your energy vibration and raising it to a higher level. Often, with this shift, there will be a powerful period of approximately three weeks where important life changes may occur. These changes are always for the highest good, though sometimes in the short term they may be uncomfortable or appear as to be chaotic, for old structures are being torn down in your life to make room for new, higher vibrations of your best self.

There are many ways to deliver this initiation, either in person or from a distance. If you want to receive a Psychic Reiki initiation that will empower you to create your own Reiki crystal, all you need to do is follow the short ritual in the following paragraphs. Traditionally in the system of Reiki, of which Psychic Reiki is a part, there is supposed to be an energy exchange in order for the initiation or healing to go to its deepest level. Typically, that is in the form of a fee paid to the Reiki master teaching the student. In this case, since the fee would typically be far more than the price of a book, what I ask of you as the form of this energy exchange is to engage in this process at the deepest level. Work on your own issues of racial bias and send Reiki to help heal and transform the hatred and ignorance that is at the seed of racism in our culture. Make this commitment with your full heart. And once you have made that commitment, engage in performing the ritual below.

★ ✦ ✺

THE PSYCHIC REIKI EMPOWERMENT

Find a place that feels comfortable for you to sit or lie down, and where you can be left alone for at least twenty minutes or longer. Then, once you are sitting or lying down, hold this book and say aloud or in your mind the following phrase, which has been energetically programmed to deliver the Psychic Reiki empowerment to you:

I would like to be empowered to use the Psychic Reiki Crystal to bring healing to myself and make the world a better place.

Then simply lie back and allow the empowerment to unfold, which generally takes only several minutes. If you are energy sensitive, you may feel the energy moving into the region in front of the center of your chest, near the heart chakra. But you may not be energy sensitive and you may feel nothing at all, which is also totally fine. Remember, feeling the energy is not actually important for the energy to do its work. You probably don't feel anything energetically when swallowing vitamins or medicine when you are ill, and yet you can see their effect in the way your health is restored. Similarly, do not put any requirement on yourself about feeling the energy in order for energy healing to work. If anything, being hyper-focused on having to feel the energy can often turn into a head trip, a mental game that has little to do with the real healing itself. Just pay attention to how you feel in the days after you do some Reiki healing on yourself. That should be the real litmus test. For now, just give gratitude and thanks for the energy itself, and know that, within the chapters to come, you will be shown how to use it for transforming your own health and the greater health of your community and the world in which we all live.

CHAPTER 18

PSYCHIC REIKI

SELF-TREATMENT

★ ✦ ✖

The focus of this book is on healing internalized racism and bringing greater healing to our world, but in sharing Psychic Reiki empowerment, I am also obligated to share the basic self-treatment. To bypass that teaching would fly in the face of my obligations as a Reiki teacher. By working on yourself on a regular basis and making yourself a better human being, you are helping to create a better world.

Begin by finding a place where you can sit or lie down comfortably. Do not attempt to perform self-treatment while driving a car, cooking in the kitchen, or doing any other externally focused activity. Since this treatment can take some people into an altered consciousness state of consciousness, it would be irresponsible to try to perform it while engaging in such activities.

Once you are comfortably seated or lying down, begin by tuning in to your Reiki crystal, which exists in front of the center of your heart. Even if you do not sense this energetic crystal, it will respond to the power of your thoughts or your voice, whichever you are more comfortable using.

Begin the session by asking your Reiki crystal to send Reiki to your brain and nervous system. Allow a few seconds for your Reiki crystal to begin honoring your request. You may notice yourself sighing or your breathing deepening, which is what often occurs for me at the start of receiving an energy healing session. After a few seconds, make another request of your Reiki crystal, since it can send Reiki to many areas simultaneously. Ask your Reiki crystal to send Reiki to your digestive system, and again notice any sensations you may experience in your body. Although I do not recommend focusing on trying to feel the energy itself, I do recommend tuning in deeply to your body and paying attention to the cues it often gives during the session, such as deeper breathing, gurgling sounds in the stomach, and releasing of tension in areas where the healing is being focused.

With the Reiki now flowing to your brain, nervous system, and digestive system, invite your Reiki crystal to send Reiki to your muscular system, including the muscles, ligaments, and tendons. Allow a few seconds for your Reiki crystal to focus the healing there. Now add another layer of healing by requesting your Reiki crystal to send Reiki to your respiratory system, which includes your lungs, sinuses, and all the airways. Again, give a few seconds for this level of the healing to begin.

Next, ask your Reiki crystal to send Reiki to your circulatory system, including your heart, veins, arteries, capillaries, and all the blood flowing throughout your body, and allow several seconds for that level of the healing to sink in. Now, invite your Reiki crystal to send Reiki to your skeletal system, including all the bones in your body, the vertebra in your spine, each of your joints, and all of the cartilage. Reiki is now flowing through several major systems in your body. Extend the healing now by asking your Reiki crystal to send Reiki to all of the major glands and major organs just to cover anything that may have been left out. At this point in the healing, Reiki is flowing throughout your entire body.

The second stage of the healing focuses on the energetic aspects of your being. Begin by inviting your Reiki crystal to send Reiki to your chakras, the seven energy centers that are integral to yoga and the Vedic healing systems. After a few seconds, invite your Reiki crystal to send Reiki to your meridians, those energetic pathways that are part of Chinese medicine and acupuncture. Once again, allow a few seconds for the healing to deepen. Next, invite your Reiki crystal to send Reiki to your mental body, that layer of your energy field in which your thought conditioning is held. This layer will become particularly important when you go deeper with techniques for healing internalized racist views, but for now, simply allow a few seconds of deepening of the healing before proceeding to the next step.

Now invite your Reiki crystal to send Reiki to your emotional body, which is another key area of focus we will explore later for deep work on transmuting buried racial bias and the emotional attachments that contribute to internalized racism. Allow a few more seconds for the healing to deepen, and then engage in the next step: invite your Reiki crystal to send Reiki to your karmic body, where your karmic conditioning is held. Allow the healing at this point to continue for as long as you wish. Your Reiki crystal is sending simultaneously to all the areas you have requested it to send healing to, and this healing should continue for several minutes.

Lie still and allow the healing to unfold for ten or fifteen minutes. Then, bring the session to a close by asking your Reiki crystal to shift all the lines of light it has been sending to become the most perfect and gentlest form of integration. When you make this request, the energy will become denser, focusing your awareness back on your physical body. Some people may even sense a slight sense of pressure in the chest as the Reiki crystal sends this denser form of Reiki energy; this is not unusual, so if you do experience it, do not be alarmed. Eventually, the Reiki crystal will simply come to close and end the healing on its own once the integration is complete, which usually happens within a couple of minutes after you request the integration. At this point, I typically give thanks to my Reiki crystal, Mikao Usui, and all the spiritual beings that made the healing possible.

Now that you have experienced self-treatment, you can use it whenever you feel the need. There are deeper aspects of this work that we will not focus on in this book, but which you can learn in my book *Psychic Reiki* (Monkfish Book Publishing Company, 2017). From this point forward, we will focus on using Psychic Reiki techniques for healing internalized racism.

CHAPTER 19

PSYCHIC REIKI TECHNIQUES

FOR HEALING INTERNALIZED

RACISM

★ ✦ ✶

Racist conditioning is like a virus to which we have all been exposed: not everyone is symptomatic, but we all carry it. Unfortunately, we can infect others with this virus through how we speak, think, and act, and even through subconscious actions like our tone of voice, eye contact (or lack thereof), and the myriad other ways in which this hideous psychological virus can express itself. My goal in writing this book is that as many individuals begin clearing their toxic racist conditioning, that conditioning will not only be contained, but that we as a culture will develop a kind of herd immunity to it and the ways in which it expresses itself in daily life. My hope is that individuals healing their internalized racism will be expressed in the overall energy of our culture, and that our culture will feel genuinely more open and accepting to people of color on a moment-to-moment basis—whether they are standing in line at the grocery store or interacting with police or other officials who represent our institutions. It is my hope that thanks to individual healings, the psychic air we all breathe will no longer be polluted by the toxic energy that has existed for hundreds of years. Perhaps I am an eternal optimist or else extremely naïve, but I do believe this will happen.

Let me share a few times in my life when my naïve belief turned out to be true. When I was in high school in the late 1970s, I wrote a paper on how one day technology would make it easier for music and film to be made in a more democratic way, how technology would evolve so that almost anyone could record an album or make a film. Several decades later, that vision has become a reality. Later on, when I was in college at the University of New Mexico in the early 1980s, in a political science class I wrote a paper predicting the peaceful downfall of the Soviet Union through internal political pressure. I was very disappointed that my paper got only a B-, but a number of years later, when the Soviet Union collapsed, I felt somewhat vindicated.

Another similar vision I have held since childhood, even while I was still immersed in a very racist environment, is that one day our society will wake up to the pain of racism and heal and transmute the web of energy that is at the root cause of racism, becoming free of it. I believe that we as a people will collectively work through our psycho-spiritual issues at a deep enough level to actually change the energetic signature of how racism manifests in our culture. And since my path of expertise is Reiki, that is the path I offer, though my hope is that other teachers in related forms of healing will use modalities like emotional freedom techniques (EFT), breathwork, art therapy, eye movement desensitization and reprocessing (EMDR), voice dialogue, family constellation work, hypnosis, and shamanic healing (to name a few) to disrupt and transmute the energetic framework of racism as it manifests inside all of us.

What follows in this chapter are a series of Psychic Reiki techniques you can use to transform and heal your own internalized racism, racist thought patterns, emotional triggers, and even any karmic conditioning you may have related to issues of race.

★　✦　✖

PSYCHIC REIKI SESSION FOR HEALING THE RACIST MINDSET

Begin this ten-step session either seated or lying down. (You will want approximately fifteen minutes or longer for the full session.) Once you are in a comfortable position, tune in to your Reiki crystal in front of the center of your chest and ask it to send Reiki to your body in the following sequence:

1) Send Reiki to the mental body, including the brain and nervous system, to clear and transform all racist thought patterns and beliefs, conscious and unconscious, on all levels of being. Wait a few seconds for this Reiki healing to start flowing from the crystal before beginning the next request.

2) Send Reiki to each cell of the body in which negative racial memories are held. Allow a few seconds for this Reiki healing to start flowing from the crystal before beginning the next request.

3) Send Reiki to the "gates of consciousness" at the base of the skull to clear all racist attachments from these two important acupuncture points where negative energy often attaches. Wait a few seconds for this

Reiki healing to start flowing from the crystal before beginning the next request.

4) Send Reiki to the emotional body to clear all racist emotions, conscious or unconscious. Allow a few seconds for this Reiki healing to start flowing from the crystal before beginning the next request.

5) Send Reiki to your chakras to release any racist energy held in each of your chakras. Wait a few seconds for this Reiki healing to start flowing from the crystal before beginning the next request.

6) Send Reiki to the meridians, the energy lines in acupuncture, to clear any energetic obstacles of racism held there. Allow a few seconds for this Reiki healing to start flowing from the crystal before beginning the next request.

7) Send Reiki to the ears to clear all racist words you have heard and to clear the energy of those words on all levels. Wait a few seconds for this Reiki healing to start flowing from the crystal before beginning the next request.

8) Send Reiki to the eyes to clear all racist stereotype images you have witnessed, whether in the media or elsewhere. Allow a few seconds for this Reiki healing to start flowing from the crystal before beginning the next request.

9) Send Reiki to all of the organs and the body's organ system, where negative racial programming may be stored at the physical level. Allow ten minutes for the healing to continue, as the Reiki crystal sends healing to all requested areas simultaneously.

10) After ten minutes have ended, ask your Reiki crystal to shift all the different lines of light that it has been sending to be for the most perfect and gentle form of integration.

I recommend using this practice two times per week at the start of your journey. Even if you are someone who considers yourself very socially aware and evolved, you may be surprised at how much is released of which you were not previously conscious.

★   ✦   ✖

PSYCHIC REIKI FOR TRANSFORMING RACIST CONDITIONING

My experience over the past few decades as an energy healer has informed me that many of our life issues are rooted in the karmic body. This session is designed to help root out negative karma that supports racist conditioning. For example, if you had a previous life in which you were taught to hate another race, that pattern of energy can likely carry over into this life, causing you to have conscious or unconscious negative feelings about another race. This session is designed to address these issues at their karmic root. This session also involves a highly advanced Psychic Reiki tool called a Reiki laser, which is an intense beam of healing light that your Reiki crystal can create between any two points in time and space.

Begin this session either seated or lying down. (You will want approximately fifteen minutes or longer for the full session.) Once you are in a comfortable position, tune in to your Reiki crystal in front of the center of your chest and ask it to send Reiki to your body in the following sequence:

1) Send Reiki to the karmic body in general. Allow a few seconds for this Reiki healing to start flowing from the crystal before beginning the next request.

2) Send Reiki to the karmic conditioning that supports any racist beliefs, racist emotions, or racist actions in this life. Wait a few seconds for this Reiki healing to start flowing from the crystal before beginning the next request.

3) Invite the Reiki crystal to create Reiki lasers through any racist karmic conditioning from the moment in time when that conditioning was first created up to the present moment. For some people, this aspect of the healing can be intense, so please allow some extra time before progressing to the next step.

4) Invite the Reiki crystal to create Reiki lasers through the ancestral lineage to clear any racist conditioning that is energetically held there. This, too, can be quite intense, so again I recommend allowing for plenty of time before moving on to the next step. Also, please note that when sending Reiki to your ancestral lines, you are actually sending it to the energetic cords between you and your ancestors, not to your ancestors as individuals. That is something I would not do unless I had specific permission from each ancestor, for which you could request by using a pendulum or other form of divination tool. Remember, always respect free will when sending Reiki, even for those who are departed.

5) Ask the Reiki crystal to shift all the lines of light that it has been sending to be for the gentlest and most perfect form of integration. In this healing you can go very deep and create profound shifts.

I recommend doing this once a week, but not more than that. It may take a few days to fully process all the energy that moves and is transformed from a session of this kind.

✶   ✦   ✶

PSYCHIC REIKI MEDITATION FOR TRANSFORMING INTERNALIZED RACISM

Your Reiki crystal has the ability to shift your own mental awareness without sending Reiki at all. This process is one I call a "Reiki meditation," in which the Divine intelligence inside the Reiki crystal simply marinates with your consciousness to create a desired shift in your conscious awareness. Reiki meditations can be quite effective in helping you to see hidden racial bias inside your own subconscious mind. These sessions can be very short or very long, as the insights that occur are beyond the bounds of time and space, so there is no time limit on how long this meditation should be. Simply allow it to unfold until you feel it is complete.

Begin this session either seated or lying down. (You will want approximately fifteen minutes or longer for the full session.) Once you are in a comfortable position, tune in to your Reiki crystal in front of the center of your chest and ask it to create a Reiki meditation in the following sequence:

1) Ask your Reiki crystal to bring you into a Reiki meditation for stillness and inner peace. This will help you feel and experience the baseline of a Reiki meditation. Allow a few seconds for the Reiki meditation to unfold between the Reiki crystal and your consciousness before beginning the next request.

2) Invite your Reiki crystal to bring you into a place of deep awareness of any racial bias, racist emotions, or racist thought patterns that still exist in your consciousness. Wait a few seconds for the Reiki meditation to unfold between the Reiki crystal and your consciousness before beginning the next request.

3) Notice what arises in your own mind: are you aware of any bias you might hold with regard to a specific race? Sometimes these insights are not about an entire race, but may be about a specific gender, age group, or even a social class of a given race. Simply pay attention and notice what arises. Remain in this Reiki meditation for as long as it feels useful and you continue having insights about yourself.

4) When the Reiki meditation feels like it has run its course, ask your Reiki crystal to perform a Reiki integration on you.

Be sure to take note of the information you received during your Reiki meditation. Think of it being like a cosmic X-ray of your own consciousness which can inform you of areas of your own hidden racial prejudice and biases that you need to transform and heal. Once you bring these issues into your awareness, you can give greater focus to the previous two Psychic Reiki sessions and tailor them to address and heal these areas inside yourself.

★ ★ ✖

PSYCHIC REIKI MEDITATION TO BE A POWERFUL ALLY

Working on your own issues of internalized racism should also include working toward being an ally for social justice. Being an ally means speaking up when you see racial injustice happening at home, on the street, or in the workplace. It also means taking active measures to help change the unjust or discriminatory laws and policies that support systemic racism in our government, businesses, and other important social institutions. You can use your Reiki crystal to assist in this process of being a true and powerful ally.

1) Ask your Reiki crystal to bring you into a Reiki meditation for stillness and inner peace. As in the previous Reiki meditation, this one is to help you feel and experience the baseline of a Reiki meditation. Allow a few seconds for this Reiki meditation to unfold between the Reiki crystal and your consciousness before beginning the next request.

2) Invite your Reiki crystal to bring you into a Reiki meditation for the courage to be the best possible ally in the fight for racial justice. Wait a few seconds for this Reiki meditation to unfold between the Reiki crystal and your consciousness before beginning the next request.

3) Notice what arises in your own mind. Do you sense actions you can take in your own life that will help promote racial justice at the local level or beyond? Simply pay attention and notice what arises. Remain in this Reiki meditation for as long as it feels useful and you continue having insights about your own courage to be an ally.

4) Now, shift away from the focus on courage and ask your Reiki crystal to bring you into a Reiki meditation for wisdom on being an ally. Wait a few seconds for this Reiki meditation to unfold between the Reiki crystal and your consciousness before beginning the next request. Notice what arises in your mind: do you sense ways you can deepen your own education on related issues? Do insights come to you about being an ally for racial justice? Simply notice and listen, allowing the wisdom of your Reiki crystal to arise in your own consciousness. Allow a few seconds for this Reiki meditation to unfold between the Reiki crystal and your consciousness before beginning the next request.

5) Invite your Reiki crystal to blend what you can take from both the courage meditation and the wisdom meditation into actionable steps for you. Listen as these steps become crystal clear in your own mind.

6) When the above step feels like it has run its course, ask your Reiki crystal to perform a Reiki integration on you.

★   ✦   ✹

There are other Psychic Reiki techniques beyond these four, but I believe too much information can actually create confusion when learning a new technique, and these four techniques alone are quite powerful. Use these four Psychic Reiki techniques on a regular basis to transform and transmute your mind, your karma, and your ancestral lineage of racist energetic imprints—and begin your journey toward freedom and promoting the freedom of others by transforming yourself into an ally for racial justice.

CHAPTER 20

THE TRANSFORMATIONAL
POWER OF SERVICE

★ ✦ ✹

Many of the world's great spiritual teachers speak of the power of selfless service to not only bring good to our communities and our world but also to show us a path for embodying love through action. Though much of this book focuses on the inner work of transforming racist conditioning from within, it is also important to remember to engage in a form of service to help manifest in the outside world what you are working to change in your inner world. Service can be as simple as committing to attending rallies focused on social justice or being active in your community at the municipal, state, and national levels to ensure that policies and laws are changed to help end systemic racism. Service also includes campaigning for a cause, asking for nothing in return, and letting your actions be guided by the love of making the world a better place, or donating time or money to causes such as Black Lives Matter, Black Girls Code, the NAACP (National Association for the Advancement of Colored People), Partnership with Native Americans, the American Indian College Fund, United We Dream, or other organizations working directly to create positive change in the world for people of color.

Service can also mean small yet powerful acts such as going out of your way to right a situation where someone is being openly discriminated against; holding a place of witnessing for the pain of another who is suffering from racial trauma; offering a smile to a stranger of another color, culture, or language; holding the door open to someone who has had many doors of opportunity closed to them in their lifetime due to the color of their skin; saying hello and honoring the humanity and presence of a person of color in a situation where you may not really even know the person; and making people of color feel welcome with any meaningful gesture of kindness that is appropriate in a given moment.

Other forms of service may include volunteering at a community center that serves a large number of people of color; a food pantry in a neighborhood that is comprised mostly of people of color; or Habitat for Humanity, which builds homes for disadvantaged populations, many of whom are people of color. The ways to serve are endless, and your choice should be guided by both your skillset as well as your passion yet also tempered by the goal of your being exposed to people who have different racial experiences than your own. Service is part of widening the web of compassion to those who do not look like you and perhaps do not speak like you. When we serve in this way, it brings us outside our cultural blinders and disrupts the brules (those bullshit rules) with which we have grown up regarding people of other races, religions, and cultures.

One way to deepen into the path of service is by creating a dedicated service journal. Buy a new journal or blank notebook to dedicate to this project. Start small by writing down an easy task that you know you can accomplish—for instance, donating money (even a small amount) to a worthy organization that focuses on positive change helping people of color; saying hello to a person of color you may not know, simply to honor their humanity; or going out of your way at work or simply in public to make a person of color feel welcome, even if just through a small act like holding open a door for that person. Each day, write down the acts of service you have performed, no matter how small. And write down your aspirations for more robust acts of service you would like to undertake. Set goals and create timelines for them to occur.

As you reflect daily in your service journal, make sure you also write about how engaging in these acts of service makes you feel. These small acts will then lead to larger acts, such as volunteering at Habitat for Humanity or a community center that primarily serves people of color. The idea is not about excluding whites from your acts of service, but that by extending that service into communities of color you can widen the lens of your own experience to share loving actions for people outside what is familiar. This creates empathy and understanding, while dissolving away prejudice, hatred and racist belief systems.

CHAPTER 21

HEALING OUR

COLLECTIVE GRIEF

✦ ✦ ✦

We explored personal grief around racism in Chapter 6. Now let's explore deeper the collective grief. We have been in a state of war for the past five hundred years—a war that includes but is not limited to violence upon indigenous cultures that have been invaded, colonized, and stripped of their lands; a war upon the feminine, on women and children as well as a disregard for the feminine aspects of the psyche, including emotions; and a war upon the earth and all of the species that inhabit it.

The level of collective grief we share about the past five hundred years is almost impossible to imagine. Most of us deny that any such grief even exists, since it cannot be proven or measured. In the Iroquois stories of the Great Peacemaker, it is told that one important aspect of bringing peace involves healing the collective grief that blocks people's ability to even hear the possibility of peace. In these stories, the grief is so enormous it has to be resolved in order for people to be able to comprehend the possibility of peace. The

Great Peacemaker smudges people's ears with sage to clear them of this grief and open them to hearing words of peace.

★　★　★

CLEARING YOUR EARS OUT OF GRIEF

Drawing upon the wisdom of the Iroquois' powerful history, write about your own grief related to the war between the races and the domination of most of the planet by Western European colonialism, which resulted in slavery, genocide, and the mass destruction of many indigenous cultures around the globe.

Begin by asking your own ears to tell you the stories you have refused to hear. Have you heard the grief of the Native Americans who died on the Trail of Tears or the grief of the slaves who were taken from their native homes in Africa, shackled and raped, beaten, or even murdered for the crime of simply wanting to be free? Imagine yourself as a young child, free from intellectualization that bypasses emotions, and write as if you are a five-year-old watching these moments in our collective history. Does it bring tears to your eyes? Does it make you want to weep deep down in your bones? Ask yourself: what do we as a culture do to honor that grief?

Write about this grief, even if you are just working it out through your imagination. You may even want to draw your grief like a child, using stick figures and symbolic images. But get the grief onto the page in some form that is authentic and meaningful. Do this as a practice, not just as a one-time event. Go deeper each time, looking anywhere inside of yourself, even into your ancestral lineage.

Start by simply asking your ancestors to write through you of things they saw, or perhaps were even part of, that may have contributed to this collective grief. Do not censor or ask if it is an actual ancestor speaking through you; rather, simply let the energy move through your pen or pencil. Go deeper and continue to write, just letting the pen move automatically, without thought of censorship. If you need at times to stop and take a breath, give yourself the freedom to do that. If you need to stop and cry, give yourself that freedom as well. Since we exist in a culture of denial around these crimes, our culture has not set up any methods of coping with this grief. To do so would be to admit that the grief exists, which would be to admit that the underlying suffering existed—that crimes against humanity occurred on a massive scale, moving across hundreds of years.

If there are places where you get stuck, dig deeper into that stuck energy. What is it about? Does it come from something you were told not to question as a child? Healing racism within is not about asking you to hate yourself, your culture, or your ancestors. It is simply about honoring the collective grief that has to date been suppressed. One thing that has remained with me on my own healing journey is a saying that was coined by Marion Weinstein, author of several books about pagan magic: "No blame and no guilt." I believe it is possible to honor the suffering and grief that happened in the course of history and simultaneously accept the responsibility of working for positive change without attributing blame and guilt. This concept also allows you to do this kind of work without fear of it turning into an exercise of racial self-hatred, which contributes nothing positive to us as individuals nor to the future of human society.

So, continue writing and digging into the grief—the things your parents never spoke about when it came to race, the things your school avoided when talking about genocide and slavery, and the immense emotional pain that is like an eclipse in the consciousness of Western civilization but of which we simply don't dare to speak.

This process of owning up to history is not about racial self-hatred, but about restoring the freedom to feel and to hope. Without these two, then there is no real process available to end the white supremacist war upon indigenous races, a war that has not even been named as a war, yet which clearly exists as one.

Once you have finished writing, whether it is a single paragraph or a hundred pages, know that there is always more to write. If you prefer some other form of expression, it doesn't have to be writing. It can be art, stick drawings, collage, poetry, dance, or music. Use the gifts you have for self-expression and take time to honor this grief in whatever form feels right to you, as long as you commit to doing it. Do it until you begin to feel open to the possibility that there can be true peace and healing between the races, where all humanity can live as one while being authentic to our collective and individual histories.

CHAPTER 22

VIOLET FLAME FOR HEALING RACIST KARMA AND RACIST CONDITIONING

✦ ✦ ✦

There are many versions of violet flame healings used by energy healers and lightworkers around the world. This powerful energy is used to transmute negative life patterns, including karmic patterns and patterns of family dysfunction that you may have inherited, including patterns of racist conditioning. Many who use the Violet Flame also work with Saint Germain, though that is not required in order for this meditation to work. If you already have a practice of connecting to the Violet Flame by working with Saint Germain or other ascended masters, go ahead and adapt your usual practice to this one below. I personally prefer to ask the Overlighting Deva of the Violet Flame—the Divine intelligence in charge of this energy—to invoke its energy around me. The Overlighting Deva of the Violet Flame is an energy you can call upon whenever you need it.

✶　✶　✶

DEEP ENERGY CLEARING WITH THE OVERLIGHTING DEVA OF THE VIOLET FLAME

For this healing, find a calm place to sit, where you will not be disturbed. Once you are seated and comfortable, close your eyes and ask the Overlighting Deva of the Violet Flame to immerse you in this powerful light for transmuting negative energy. Say aloud, or in your mind, the following invocation:

> *I ask the Overlighting Deva of the Violet Flame to activate a sphere of the Violet Flame surrounding me in all directions six feet in diameter.*

(Allow a few seconds for this to manifest.)

> *I ask the Overlighting Deva of the Violet Flame to purge all racist conditioning from my mental body using this sacred light.*

(Allow several seconds for this work to begin manifesting.)

> *I ask the Overlighting Deva of the Violet Flame to release all racist conditioning, all racist hatred and bias from my emotional body using this sacred light*

(Allow several seconds for this level of the work to unfold.)

I ask the Overlighting Deva of the Violet Flame to infuse the Violet Flame into my karmic body and release all karmic conditioning that supports racist behavior, racist thoughts and racist emotions

(Allow another several seconds for this level of work to unfold.)

I ask the Overlighting Deva of the Violet Flame to fill each cell of my body with the Violet Flame, to purge all race-based trauma from the cells of my body.

(Allow a few seconds for this work to manifest in your body.)

I ask the Overlighting Deva of the Violet Flame to send the Violet Flame through my ancestral lines to purge and release all racist conditioning, all racist belief systems, and all racial bias, both conscious and unconscious, to free me from any negative influence from my ancestors on issues of race.

(Allow a few seconds for this to manifest in your ancestral lines.)

I ask the Overlighting Deva of the Violet Flame to send the Violet Flame to any remaining areas where my racist conditioning, racist belief systems, and racial bias conscious and unconscious exist in my energy field or physical body, on any dimension and all levels of existence to free me from any negative racist influences.

(Allow a few seconds for this part of the healing to unfold.)

Now, give thanks to the Overlighting Deva of the Violet Flame for the healing you have just received. Continue repeating this process on a weekly basis.

CHAPTER 23

THE POWER OF FASTING

AND PRAYER

✦ ✦ ✦

The spiritual power of fasting is noted in most of the world's spiritual traditions and is said to help remove even the greatest of obstacles when combined with prayer. One does not need to be aligned with a religion to fast or pray. Fasting for many can be part of a regular health regimen. And prayer can be simply asking the universe, higher self, and the intelligence of all life to help you. It does not have to be a traditional religious prayer to be prayerful. In fact, asking with your own heart in many ways can be more authentic and more powerful.

There have been two notable times in my own spiritual healing journey when I fasted and prayed to arrive at an outcome that had otherwise alluded me. The first time was when I was trying to get out of a dysfunctional business partnership, where I loved the business itself, but dreaded my partner, who had an unhealthy and unrequited romantic attachment to me. I had been trying for months to get out of that situation but could not free myself, when I was told by my dear shaman friend and mentor Carolion to fast for three days, eating only fruit and drinking only water, and that I also should ask Spirit for guidance.

So, for three days I ate only fruit, which felt very cleansing to me, and drank only water. Several days after doing this, I had a flash of spiritual guidance that moved me hundreds of miles away, where I was immediately given my first job at Omega Institute. The business ended up going entirely to my business partner, but I was suddenly free from a horrible situation.

The second time I engaged in fasting and prayer, it was five years later and I was in a far more serious situation in which I felt that my own life and sanity were on the line. I had disturbed some sacred territory while traveling in Bali, and for months afterward, my entire life seemed to be collapsing around me. Not only did I have vivid visions of my own death almost every time I closed my eyes, but all my friends suddenly abandoned me, animals acted strangely when they were near me, my girlfriend at the time cheated on me and broke my heart, and everything I did seemed to go wrong. It was as if I had been cursed.

Now, I don't really think I was cursed, but I was certainly paying a heavy price for my own spiritual arrogance: I had trespassed upon a sacred site in Bali, even though I meant no harm. I knew I needed to atone for my transgression, and I was advised by my mentor Carolion to fast again, but this time for fourteen days, and also offer ceremonial prayers. So I decided that while I fasted, I would also write a novel about the painful time I'd been having since that moment of transgression in Bali, and dedicate the book to the spirits I had offended.

I was living in a youth hostel in Montreal at the time, and each day I wrote in the hostel's common room, visible to the other guests, and ate only fruit, drank only water, and did ceremonial prayer while hiding near a bunkbed for privacy. I felt a little stronger every day, with my sanity returning, and it seemed like everything was going well until my last day in Montreal. That day, after I finished the last few lines of the novel and clicked the save button on my 1995 IBM Thinkpad, I watched the blue bar stretch across the screen indicating that my document was being saved—but when the blue bar went away the whole document was blank. I was stunned. I asked a friend I'd made at the hostel who had just accepted a job at McGill University's computer science department, to come take a look. He dug through my computer files for almost an hour, getting more and more frustrated.

"It weird," he told me. "I have been watching you work on your novel every day since I've been here, and yet when I go into the files of your computer it seems you haven't written anything for weeks."

My book was to be an offering to the spirits of Bali, and they had taken it. In return, my life came back. The next day, old friends began emailing me. I was offered my seasonal job back at Omega Institute, and though my broken romantic relationship didn't heal, everything else in my shattered life suddenly became whole again. I attribute that to the power of fasting and prayer—a prayer which, in this instance, was in the form of the novel I wrote as an offering.

I don't fast often, but I know there are many ways to fast and to do so effectively. If you are well versed in the spiritual art of fasting or have a healthy fasting practice that works for you, feel free to adapt the version I am offering, which is a simple fruit fast.

★ ★ ✖

FASTING TO DETOX FROM RACISM

Begin with committing to fasting. A twenty-four-hour fast is simple and attainable. Choose a date to begin the fast, typically starting in the morning and lasting until the following morning. (You can start in the midday or evening, as long as you intend to go a full twenty-four-hour cycle.) Once you have made the commitment, plan accordingly. Avoid making social commitments that would distract you from the fast or make it unusually difficult.

Hold your intention that the fast will detox you of racist toxins in all forms—emotional, mental, political, social, and karmic. If you have a specific spiritual practice that works for you, feel free to weave it into the fast, but even if you have no specific spiritual practice, the fast can still work. Simply hold the intention that the intelligence in each cell of your body is releasing the illness of racism on all levels during the fast; tell this to your mind, and your body will know it.

Each time you eat during the fast, eat slowly and mindfully. Imagine that as you are chewing your food and breaking it down, it is transforming into spiritual medicine. If you have a specific spiritual practice, you can bless the food in accordance with that tradition. But if you are atheist or agnostic, just use intention and your imagination, and the effect on your body and mind will still occur.

Whenever you take a sip of water during the fast, intend that it is cleansing you from the inside out, washing each cell of your body free from any racial hatred or bias, known or unknown. You can dedicate your fast to serve all who will benefit from it, including other souls who may be ancestors in your lineage. The fast will create a sense of empty space inside of you, which you can think of as being space for new possibilities.

Once you complete your fast to detox from racism, consider when you would like to repeat it. Perhaps you can commit to fasting once per month, or maybe you'll consider fasting for longer than a single day.

Repeat the practice in a way that works for you. Do whatever feels right, keeping in mind that this is not a competition, but a practice. Making a practice work for you is far better than striving for an unattainable goal and then coming away from that feeling like a failure. If you feel confident with fasting for a single day after the first few times you do it, you may want to invite others to join you. Sharing your fasting intention with others can make you feel more committed. It can also be a noninvasive way to invite others to question their own inner racism, which we all share, since we live in a racially toxic environment. Without blame or guilt, you can help yourself and others begin to heal, simply by being mindful of what you put into your body.

Extend that mindfulness to consider what you, and our society, have been putting into your mind and heart since you were a very small child. Even if fasting serves no other purpose, it can remind you to be thoughtful about what you are becoming and what is becoming you, because we are what we eat, as well as what we read and what we watch in the media.

CHAPTER 24

THE MAHARISHI EFFECT

★ ✦ ✹

The Maharishi Effect is the concept that individual consciousness, especially when directed toward a specific conscious outcome, can influence collective consciousness for positive change.
It is named after the Indian guru Maharishi Mahesh Yogi, who
claimed in the 1960s that one percent of a population practicing
Transcendental Meditation (TM) would positively impact the local
environment. By doing our own inner work, whether it is through
energy healing, writing, meditation, art, or some other practice, we
can impact the world around us. By doing the practices in this book,
you can create internal and external change, but you can focus that
even deeper with specific intention and practice. Here are some
meditations and techniques you can use to send healing light out
into the world to transform our collective consciousness.

★ ✦ ✹

THE SOCIAL JUSTICE ALTAR AND BLESSING

Begin by a creating an altar to social justice, where you can focus healing out into the world to bring unity and racial healing. On the altar, which can be arranged on any surface such as a tabletop or shelf, place images that inspire you, including perhaps a photograph of Dr. Martin Luther King Jr. and/or other transformational leaders in the fight for racial equality and justice. Add other symbolic images such as flags or a photo of the earth. Make your altar personal to you, adding any images that inspire you spiritually—perhaps religious symbols or images such as angels, saints, power animals, or whatever image that symbolizes a higher power for you. Even if you are an atheist or agnostic, you can use photos of the forces of nature to represent the power of the universe such as the ocean, mountains, planets, stars, or the sun and the moon.

Use any images that create for you the sense of an awesome and benevolent power greater than yourself. Once you have collected these images, add some crystals such as selenite, which has the property of clearing negative energy, and rose quartz, which has the property of opening the heart. Be creative and allow your own intuition to be your most important guide. Also add to your altar something to bring focus, such as a candle or an incense burner. Being able to focus on a flame or the single point of a burning incense stick is powerful for focusing the mind into a deep and meditative state.

When you have finished creating your altar using all the above items, create a blessing of intention for it by lighting your candle or incense and saying the following words or something similar:

By the powers which made this universe, I hereby consecrate this altar for sending healing and unity consciousness out into the world to disrupt the racist mindset as it exists in human consciousness and replace it with unity and love. I manifest this now, so be it!

Once you have consecrated your altar, you can go to it anytime with the intention of bringing racial healing to humanity. Below are several prayers and meditations you can use to deepen your practice of sending healing out to the world on this issue; the first one is an adaptation of one of the Psychic Reiki techniques from Chapter 19.

★　★　★

SENDING REIKI TO THE OVERSOUL OF HUMANITY

Begin by standing or sitting before your altar. (You will want approximately fifteen minutes or longer for the full session.) This technique involves sending Reiki to the Oversoul of Humanity, and not to specific individuals, as that is something I would not do without a person's consent. The Oversoul of Humanity can be compared to the body of humanity, to which you as an individual have the right to bring healing since you are like a cell within that body.

Once you are in a comfortable position, tune in to your Reiki crystal in front of the center of your chest and ask it to send Reiki to the following sequence:

1) Send Reiki to the mental body of the Oversoul of Humanity to clear racist thought patterns and beliefs, whether conscious and unconscious, on all levels of being. Wait a few seconds for this Reiki healing to start flowing from the crystal before beginning the next request.

2) Send Reiki to all land and buildings where negative racial memories are held. Then allow a few seconds for this Reiki healing to start flowing from the crystal before beginning the next request.

3) Send Reiki to the spiritual body of the Oversoul of Humanity to clear all racist spiritual beliefs. Wait a few seconds for this Reiki healing to start flowing from the crystal before beginning the next request.

4) Send Reiki to the emotional body of the Oversoul of Humanity to clear all racist emotions, conscious or unconscious. Allow a few seconds for this Reiki healing to start flowing from the crystal before beginning the next request.

5) Imagine the world in a place of racial unity and harmony and ask your Reiki crystal to send Reiki to empower that vision. Allow several seconds for this Reiki healing to start flowing from the crystal before beginning the next request.

Remember that your Reiki crystal is sending simultaneously to all the recipients you have named. Allow this to go for at least ten minutes. In my experience, some people can become ungrounded with this type of work and need to make sure they integrate afterwards, so be sure to ask your Reiki crystal to perform a Reiki integration on you as an individual and on the Oversoul of Humanity simultaneously, shifting all of the various lines of light it has been sending to be for the most perfect and gentle form of integration for you as well as the Oversoul of Humanity.

★ ✦ ✶

I recommend using this practice as a weekly ritual. The more healing light you and others send, focusing on sending Reiki out into the world for racial healing, the more the outside world will be impacted by the Maharishi Effect.

★　★　★

HEALING THE WORLD WITH LOVE

Another simple meditation you can perform in front of your altar is to visualize in present time a world that is overflowing with love and harmony between the races—an authentic love that embraces rather than denies the pain and suffering of the past five hundred years. Use your imagination to see this in clear detail, perhaps focusing on integrated neighborhoods or people of different races joining hands celebrating the end of the five-hundred-year race war. See the world as you imagine it could be, as if there is a vision board in your mind for a world in complete racial unity and harmony. What does that look like? Allow this vision to move out through your breath, over your altar, and out into the world. Practice this technique a few minutes each day, to set a tone for a new world within you and in the world beyond.

REPARATIONS

★ ✦ ✗

When I was a child, one technique I used to soothe myself whenever I was being psychologically tormented, sexually violated, or subjected to other forms of soul torture was to imagine that I was seeing my life from the moon or a far-off planet. I would imagine seeing my life from such a great distance that the pain of what I was experiencing on earth didn't seem able to hurt me. I could witness my pain, but I could also see the oceans and the beauty of the whales, the mountains, and the joy happening among people in other places—and this universal perspective allowed me to survive what was happening to me.

Sometimes I try the same technique to examine racism by imagining a particular situation to be happening on some imaginary island. That takes the charge out of whatever is happening and allows me to see it more clearly. Below is an example of how to use this technique.

★ ✦ ✗

PAYING REPARATIONS

Imagine three islands. You can name them whatever you wish. On one island, there is a lot of war, fear, and strife, so some of the people on that island decide to move to the second island. That island has robust resources, and its native inhabitants live close to nature, so the invading islanders kill off most of the natives and steal their land.

The invaders from the first island then steal the inhabitants of the third island and enslave them through threat of death to work on the second island that has been conquered, replacing that island's native population, which has mostly been slaughtered.

This process goes on for a few hundred years, until the enslaved people finally attain some degree of freedom. They can own things, just not too much and not in certain areas. They have services that are inferior in terms of health, education, and housing, but they are expected to accept that and not protest, lest they be killed as troublemakers.

As the generations continue, the original inhabitants of the second island are given smaller and smaller portions of land in which to exist and are nearly driven to insanity. The descendants of the enslaved people who were stolen from their original homeland on the third island, and who have provided the labor for the second island to be one of the wealthiest islands ever, are still treated poorly most of the time.

Eventually the descendants of the invaders, who originally came from the war-torn first island but now rule the rich second island, start to notice how hard it is to keep their ideals about freedom, equality, and the pursuit of happiness. It makes them feel unhappy to think about how poorly their ancestors behaved. So rather than pay the enslaved people's descendants the amount that is owed them for their slave labor and come clean about the wrongs that were done, the invaders' descendants instead leave a breadcrumb trail of minute offerings to the original inhabitants. Whenever an occasional riot erupts, a few more breadcrumbs are tossed, but nothing really changes. The descendants of the first, war-torn island still hold all the power, and they are even able to use science to take themselves up to the moon and back. But whenever any of the descendants of the original inhabitants or the enslaved people asks for reparations, they claim that would be too hard to figure out, and anyway, how could they ever afford to pay them?

This is how my innocent inner child sees the issue of paying reparations to Black and Native American descendants: as an obvious thing that should happen, but one which will be argued against until the collective heart of the original invaders is healed. I am sure some will say my argument is sophomoric, but sometimes sophomoric, innocent eyes are the only ones that can see the truth.

CHAPTER 26

RESOLUTION

★ ★ ✖

found out just how deep my healing journey would go when I was visiting Santa Fe, New Mexico, in September 2004. I did not want to attend a training there with my mentor, Alexandra Marquardt, as I had been living in New York State for some time by then, and I had not returned to New Mexico, where my family still lived, for over a decade. The last time I had been there, I'd spent most of my time on the floor of a friend's apartment, holding onto my head to fend off migraine headaches I was experiencing from being in the same city where many of the atrocities I'd experienced as a child had happened.

I wanted so much to avoid ever returning to New Mexico again that I had even tried to talk Alexandra into moving the training to another city in another state—anything so long as I didn't have to go back to New Mexico. But she didn't agree with me.

"It will be good for you," Alexandra insisted. "Please come to the training."

In the end I took her advice, though I still felt nervous. When I arrived at the airport in New Mexico, I felt jittery. I had experienced a lot of healing since the last time I'd been there, but I had an underlying feeling of fear even though I did sense I was not going to end up on the floor holding my head again this time. I took pride in the healing to which I had dedicated myself for more than a decade, and I could feel the results of it as I stood looking out at the gorgeous mountains touching the deep blue New Mexican sky, knowing they were the very same mountains I had seen each day as a child.

During the training, which lasted for over a week, I worked deep into my karmic body, bringing in Divine light to heal the trauma and conditioning that still existed there. I had healed so much over the years through shamanic journeys, soul retrievals, art therapy, support groups, Gestalt, twelve-step work, Reiki, and Wiccan magical rituals in which I had engaged almost daily for more than ten years. But this time I was going even deeper, like a runner who is coming into the final mile of a long marathon race. There would always be more healing to do, more metaphorical races to run, but this race was coming to an end, and I could feel it.

One day during the training, while sending Divine light into my karmic body, I felt what I can only describe as a puff of smoke move up along my spine, and then out of the top of my head. This energetic smoke was yellow and felt as if it were contaminated with old toxins which I had been carrying between me and my biological family for several lifetimes. After it moved out of my body, I mentioned this experience to Alexandra; I told her the puff of energetic smoke came out of me like pollution through a smokestack.

"I feel I can go home now," I said. "I feel like I could go to the places where I grew up and it won't bother me anymore."

"I believe that you can," she said, smiling as if to remind me of that telephone conversation we had had months before, when she convinced me to attend the training even though it was happening in New Mexico.

That night there was a celebration in Santa Fe—the Burning of Zozobra, a cultural ritual that has taken place for hundreds of years. Zozobra is the Spanish word for anxiety, worry, and sinking, and is presented in effigy as a huge puppet, about sixty feet tall, of an old man who is also called Old Man Gloom. In New Mexico, the annual ritual burning of Zozobra is extremely festive, with music and dancing taking place while the puppet moves and points toward the audience while its groans are amplified through enormous audio speakers.

I had grown up knowing about this ritual, but I never had attended it. Our training was taking place in a beautiful hotel complex that featured luxurious individual units, a swimming pool, and a classroom. The complex was located on a hill with a direct sightline of the field where the Burning of Zozobra was happening. In the early evening, before the festivities began, I sat on a bench, using some of the new energy healing tools I had learned at the training. I wove threads of Divine light directly between me and the Zozobra puppet, intending that when Zozobra was set afire, that the power of the flame would also burn out of me all the residual pain from my childhood trauma. I also wove the thread of Divine light into the earth, intending that it should go from Zozobra all the way back to my childhood home in New Mexico, and burn all my painful memories of that place out of its walls, floor, and ceiling.

As I sat on the bench for an hour or more, moving my hands to distribute the Divine light, other students came by and asked me what I was doing. I told them I was just doing some healing, not wanting to go into the details of my personal magic ritual on that powerful night. I sat there until darkness fell, listening to the music coming from the field and watching the dancing and spinning of fire, all the while intending that the old toxins would finally and forever be purged from me.

When the flames were lit and the sounds of Zozobra's moaning rose, I started coughing, as if all that old emotional poison was being ripped out of me. As I watched the scene below, I could feel the pain of my childhood being consumed. At certain points, it felt as if entire energetic structures in my mind were falling the way the frame of a house collapses in a fire. I could feel myself being restructured inside—and all the while, the whole of Santa Fe was dancing in a wild and festive party in the fields below where I sat.

That night I slept deeply, as if I were finally, actually cleansed, in a way I had never been before, of the events that had haunted my whole life.

When the training ended several days later, rather than take the shuttle to the airport, I got a ride there with my friend Denise, who had rented a car to attend the training with Alexandra, and would be flying home to California. As we approached the airport, I saw we were far ahead of schedule, and I asked her if she would consider driving me past the home where I had grown up, a place I had feared going for many years. Denise agreed, so I gave her the address.

As we began the drive, there were no changes in my breathing, no headaches, no old emotional baggage arising. When we turned off the interstate for my neighborhood, I still felt calm and at ease, but I wasn't sure if that feeling would last. We turned a few more times near the rectangular park, bordered with elm trees, where I had played as a child, and where I had hidden in a cement tunnel to avoid my family. We parked across the street from my old home, directly across from the sycamore tree I used to pound with a baseball bat to release my childhood rage. From across the street, I could see the wound I had pounded into its bark so many years ago with my Louisville Slugger. I was happy to see the tree had not only endured but had grown huge and thrived.

There it was: the old stucco house, painted green, where I had been subjected to many horrors as a child. Yet I felt entirely neutral and peaceful, as if I was simply looking at a glass of water; I saw the clarity of my childhood with no emotional charge, no pain, no suffering at all. I didn't know who lived in that house now, nor did it seem important to go find out. Being directly across the street from the house was enough to confirm for me that my healing was complete and I could move on to the next chapter of my life.

I share this story to show that it is possible to wipe clean levels of pain that are unimaginable. It is possible to claw your way back to sanity using things like energy healing and other spiritual practices. They may not be the medicine that works for everyone, but for many they take the healing far beyond what is traditionally possible.

The exercises and information in the previous chapters of this book can heal you if you open to that possibility. And if enough of us heal the residual racist toxins inside us—the toxins created by a trajectory of history that has lasted more than five hundred years—then that healing will expand to society as a whole. It will be felt in daily interactions, when we no longer cross the street out of fear of a Black man and when a policeman no longer fires his weapon at an innocent person based on a kneejerk cultural reaction. This healing is possible, I believe. All I am asking is for you to believe with me that we can transcend the greatest of horrors, both individually and collectively, if only we try moving forward with baby steps and take the work where it needs to go.

In closing, I offer one last dedication, to the Black man I saw shot down many years ago, and whose name I do not know. May his spirit offer me forgiveness for my family's crimes and help carry this book wherever it needs to go to bring greater healing to our world.

A REALITY SHOW
GONE WRONG

★ ✦ ✶

On January 6, 2021 I saw my father and his racist murderous friend Clyde on television invading the United States Capitol during the Trump-incited insurrection. I didn't see them literally, not their actual faces, but I saw their actions, their mindset, their berserker rage. It was the same vibration of energy I witnessed daily as a child.

I saw anew Clyde's fascination with conspiracy theories, the pathetic "Gemstone File" that he'd circulated around my father's store—a poorly written fantasy claiming Aristotle Onassis had paid an assassin to murder John F. Kennedy so he could marry Jackie Kennedy. Since it was typed on paper, Clyde assumed it was an official government report that had somehow been leaked to the public, and therefore absolutely true. I was only a kid but when he handed me that report, I knew immediately that it was clearly absent of any evidence, logic, or truth; yet to Clyde and the others who worked for my father, it was real as the evening news. After all, it was typed on paper!

If Clyde and my father are still alive today, they are no doubt followers of QAnon, the discredited and disproven conspiracy theory claiming there is a secret ring of Satan-worshipping, cannibalistic, anti-Trump, pedophile Democrats. This is especially strange, given that Clyde himself was a pedophile who got caught by his wife molesting their two-year-old granddaughter. (And yet, afterwards he remained welcome at my father's store, and he never spent a day behind bars for any of the crimes he committed, for he was protected by a culture of lies that always bent the truth to protect people like him.)

As I watched the insurrection unfold on television, I noticed that Blue Lives Matter flags were being carried by the very mob that was attacking, injuring, and even killing one of the police who were trying to defend the US Capitol. The irony of this was striking. The American flag symbolizes our democracy, and the Blue Lives Matter flag, essentially an American flag with a blue stripe across the middle, clearly symbolizes our country being riven in two. It symbolizes a nation divided, and it was waved proudly both by counter-protestors at Black Lives Matter protests in the summer of 2020 as well as by the insurrectionist mob on January 6. Seeing this flag carried into the US Capitol deepened my belief that the Blue Lives Matter movement has never really been about defending the police—it is actually an insidious racist technique for devaluing the Black Lives Matter movement and silencing people who protest police brutality toward people of color.

The insurrectionists conveyed the power of lies being repeated. The repetition of these lies—like any affirmation, prayer, or mantra—increases their power. In this case, that power was used to destroy and kill.

I was born into a similar system of lies: lies that protected murderers, pedophiles, and white supremacists; lies that created the illusion that my world was somehow normal, okay, something I should adapt to, something I didn't even need to consider cruel.

When cruelty is normalized, evil flourishes. I experienced this in many ways while growing up. Sometimes, when my father was drunk, he played a strange game with my brother and me. He would offer to give us each a hundred-dollar bill for every hair he could pull from our toes using a small tweezer. But he never actually pulled out the hair, he merely tugged at it slowly until my older brother or I could no longer stand the pain and called off the game before ever getting our hundred dollars. Every time, we were tricked by our father, who simply wanted to watch us experience both physical pain and the humiliation of not receiving prize money we knew could easily have been ours if we had just let him pull the hair out entirely.

January 6, 2021 was a reality show gone wrong. For me, it meant seeing my family's lies, deceptions, mind games, anger, rage, and racist venom all spattered across the television screen at once. My father may not have been there in the flesh, but he was there in the spirit of the man who wore a shirt celebrating Camp Auschwitz. My father often spoke of wanting to erect a statue of Hitler in front of his store to terrify and frighten away people of Jewish descent.

I had seen the insurrection before as a child—and even though what I'd experienced was on a smaller scale, it was just as violent and no less frightening than what I saw on January 6. And I could easily have become one of those US Capitol insurrectionists.

Many times while growing up I wanted to explode, to give in to the darkness boiling inside of me. In fifth grade, I sat next to a boy called Seth, and we sort of became friends. In our spare time we drew detailed scenes of warfare on sheets of paper, taping them together to extend like a long scroll. We were elevated to hero status when our teacher invited us to tape that scroll of war and rage along the walls of our classroom. What kind of education was that? What could children learn by glorifying tanks, bombs, and machine guns in the temple of an elementary school classroom?

But our drawings were part of the America I knew—the America I was taught to be proud of, and to obey. Seth and I drew many of our war scenes after school in his living room, where a KKK hood hung on the wall as if it were a work of art. He told me, without any sense of shame or embarrassment, that the hood had belonged to his grandfather. "It's part of my family heritage," he said.

The honest truth was that I didn't like Seth. He cheated and lied constantly. But I didn't have any other friends, and I understood him—he fit into the environment I already knew. Plus, spending time at Seth's house allowed me to escape the abuse that awaited me at home and gave me a respite from kids like Steven, the boy who sat next to me in chorus, who punched me in the arm whenever the teacher wasn't looking and terrified me. One day I hammered nails into a board and slipped it inside my coat sleeve, ready for Steven to punch me again. I yearned to hear his scream echo through the classroom when his hand got punctured by the board of nails hidden up my sleeve. But that day he left me alone, as if he could sense my malicious plan.

When I look at images of the frenzied insurgents, I see terrorists, white supremacists, and cowards. Yet, in those images I also see who I might have become. *Tat Tvam Asi:* That otherness is myself. To dance above my ancestral history without ever feeling any of it, or not to experience the rot and stench of its aroma, is not worthy of who I wish to be. I am the son of incest. I am the son of rape. My child's eyes witnessed race-based murder. I am the son of a slippery, well-educated hatred that slithers away from addressing America's five hundred years of enslaving other people—and this hatred has an honest face and a heartfelt human voice.

Please know I am not anti-white. I am simply pro-human. The most elevated form of whiteness is a whiteness that has fully faced itself in the mirror, not in self-hatred, but in seeking liberation by stripping down naked before God and Goddess and saying, "This is what I am, and this is why I weep, and this is what I can redeem, and this is the light inside of me opening now for healing"—and say all that with the heart of a child.

And if I, as an individual, can return home to my body, sane from the journey I have known in this life, then so can anyone who is willing to shuck the garment of lies so many of us have worn for the past five hundred years and weave a new way of seeing, a new way of being, harnessing all the wisdom and healing opportunities that exist for anyone who is willing to open their eyes and see them. By doing this, we can change the world for the better, for anyone and everyone, regardless of their race, culture, gender, and beliefs. We can be open to the heartbeat of humanity and let it dance through us all, the way it is meant to be.

—*Brett Bevell*

ACKNOWLEDGMENTS

★ ✦ ✹

I want to thank Amma (Mata Amritanandamayi) for her light, which guided me to write this book, and express deep gratitude to Dr. Dore Bowen, who helped guide me through the very vulnerable terrain of my master's thesis many years ago, which gave birth to many of the initial ideas of this book. I would also like to thank Ji Hyang Padma and Gina Harris for their tireless dedication to creating innovative programs that address issues of racism at Omega Institute, and for the conversations we have had there, which helped inspire me to write this book.

Many thanks to Vishen Lakhiani: Through his books and the founding of his company Mindvalley, he has inspired me to believe holistic education can and will transform humanity on such a grand scale that it will change the trajectory of human history. Similarly, I want to thank Klemen Struc for the conversations we have had about using energy healing to create social transformation by impacting human consciousness at a massive level through apps and worldwide events on the internet. Those conversations also helped spawn this work.

And finally, I want to acknowledge my wife Helema for all her insights about race, and the humor with which those insights have been delivered.

Reiki master Brett Bevell is the author of several books, including *Psychic Reiki, The Wizard's Guide to Energy Healing, The Reiki Magic Guide to Self-Attunement*, and *Reiki for Spiritual Healing*. He teaches regularly at premier holistic venues and offers energy healing through the Soulvana App by Mindvalley. As a poet and performance artist, Bevell is also the author of two long narrative poem books *America Needs a Woman President* and *America Needs a Buddhist President*, which initially aired on National Public Radio's *All Things Considered*. Bevell has entertained audiences around the world with his live oral recitations.

CPSIA information can be obtained
at www.ICGtesting.com
Printed in the USA
LVHW030002041021
699410LV00003B/3